soccer games for kids

Dedicated by Osvaldo Garcia:
    To my daughter Sandra and my son Alejandro.
Dedicated by Kevin Coffey:
    To Timmy King.

SOCCER GAMES FOR KIDS

Osvaldo S. Garcia

Illustrated by Kevin P. Coffey

Translated from the Spanish
by Marta Espinoza and Linda Weitzman

CHRONICLE BOOKS   **SAN FRANCISCO**

CIP

Printed in the United States of America.
Library of Congress Cataloging in Publication Data
Garcia, Osvaldo S.
Soccer games for kids.
1. Soccer—Juvenile literature. 2. Ballgames—Juvenile
literature. I. Coffey, Kevin. II. Title.
GV943.25.G33   796.33'42   78-20821
ISBN 0-87701-133-8

Book and cover design by John Beyer.
Cover photograph by Jean McMann.
Composition by Media Etcetera.

Chronicle Books/870 Market Street/San Francisco, CA 94102

Contents

Introduction

The main purpose of this book is to help you to play soccer for the fun of it. But while you are having fun you can also learn that this sport can be of benefit to the mind as well as to the body. I want to suggest something ambitious in these days when many people believe that some sort of psychological therapy must be the answer to all of our problems: What if we simply have a little fun in a group sport? I think you'll find that many of your tensions will disappear after a good game.

This applies both to children and to adults. I know I've had fun in this way and have concluded that there is nothing more beautiful than putting on my soccer shoes and inviting my son to come out and play awhile. I think that the best way for me to handle my own stress and anxieties is to take my son by one hand, to grab a ball with the other and go to the park and play. The way that playing soccer has affected me is that (although my appetite is better) I have lost weight — and I have become a more tolerant person.

I am continually surprised to discover the importance that sport has in the lives of people — both adults and children. But my book isn't designed to explore the depths of the human soul. My goal is simple: I wish to give you some tips on playing soccer in the hope that they will help you to have more fun.

This book is designed for parents, coaches, and teachers who will help children play together and learn the techniques that will improve their skills. But this book can also be used by kids themselves who organize their own teams and play on the schoolyard or in the park on weekends. There are games for young children who are learning the basic skills of moving the ball and guarding an opponent, as well as making goals. My objective is to give directions for the game plays that are the most fun and rewarding for your group.

It's always a good idea to start any activity slowly. After the first day on the field muscles will be aching, tendons and ligaments will need to be stretched and limbered up. The best way to begin is to choose a game that you can play for the fun of it. Go to the park and play it until you are very familiar with its plays. Don't think about it as "exercise." And don't take it too seriously. When you tire of that game, find another one. All of these games have been designed to help you improve your individual abilities and show you how to develop certain techniques.

But don't forget: Have fun!

Chapter One

LET'S START

To begin playing soccer the only thing that you really need is a ball. It doesn't even have to be a regulation soccer ball — its only requirement is that it be round and that it bounce. When I was a child my friends and I would go out and play the games in this book with a ball that we made out of old nylons. We called it "rag ball" and in the 1930s and 1940s rag ball was so popular that almost all the players that Argentina produced began their careers playing with this type of ball.

What's Needed

You can learn with whatever type of ball that you happen to have. And soccer is a game where a person's weight, height, or physical strength is of little importance. The most important thing to have as you begin to play is the desire to learn to play well. It's very nice to work with high-quality sports equipment but just having it is no guarantee that it alone will produce good results.

Of all the balls that you can buy at the sporting goods store there is only one that we will call "regulation." It is available in three sizes:

Number 3 — circumference: 23½ to 25 inches; weight: 10 to 12 ounces.

Number 4 — circumferences: 25 to 26½ inches; weight: 12 to 14 ounces.

Number 5 — circumferences: 27 to 28 inches; weight 14 to 16 ounces. Number 5 is the size ball used regularly throughout the world. Number 4 is good to use for children who are under twelve years. Number 3 is advisable for those eight years or younger.

Once you've got the ball all you have to do is select a place where you can play. Soccer is played throughout the world on natural grass. And real grass is without a doubt the best thing in the world to practice on. This doesn't mean you can't play on concrete, in a gym, or even on beach sand or Astroturf. Most places will do because, as you begin to play, you will probably forget all about the surface or any other obstacles that may at first seem a hindrance.

The Place

Choose as open a space as possible because the lack of obstructions will help eliminate the risk of injury. Avoid playing where there may be columns or trees or other objects that you might not pay attention to when running down the field. Search the area carefully for ditches or sprinklers that might be hidden in the grass. If you find potholes fill them in with sand. Make certain that the area directly in front of the goal is the flattest that you can find since it is the area that will get the most traffic.

Don't play near cars. Often you will be concentrating so hard on the play and the ball that you won't be aware of the danger of passing traffic. If good soccer is to be played, you should take the weather and its effect on the players into consideration. Climate — including heat, humidity, and the dampness of the grass after a rain — is an important factor. If the ground is slippery, accidents could easily happen and it might be best to postpone playing until the conditions are better. If you are playing indoors make certain that the windows of the gym or playroom are well protected.

With a little imagination any material can be used to provide yourself with the equipment you'll need to play soccer. These are the common materials and they will be of good use to you in setting up the game: *Chalk or rope.* To mark the playing field I recommend chalk but many people prefer a rope that has been staked into the ground or onto the floor (see Fig. 1). If you do use a rope, it can be easily removed after you've finished the game.

Equipment

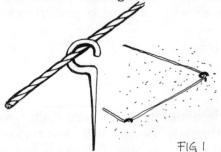

FIG 1

Stakes. These should measure 5 feet in height. I've used stakes made of wood that are 1½ inches wide and are painted white so that they are easier for the players to see. You can also flag them to make them more visible.

Cones. These are very useful for many purposes, such as marking corners, providing obstacles for dribbling drills, and forming goal boundaries. They are easy to use because they are portable. You'll need at least four cones for the game drills here.

Goals. In some game drills small goals are used in place of the larger ones. In these instances no goalies are necessary to protect the goal because the drill is designed so that the players shoot directly into the goal. This type of goal serves a valuable purpose: it retains all the

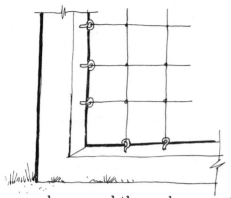
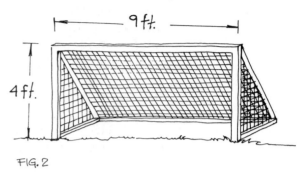

FIG. 2

men as players and those players get practice in playing and shooting without interruption. This type of goal can be made inexpensively by just about anyone who has had some experience with carpentry. I suggest using 2x4s painted white in front. The rest of the goal can be painted red. (See Fig. 2.)

Uniforms. All that is really required for a uniform is a T-shirt, shorts, socks, and shoes. I suggest that the shirt and socks be cotton because it stays fresh in the summer and is warm in the winter. To protect your feet you may want to wear two pairs of socks. Soccer shoes are not absolutely necessary; most professional soccer players wear regular tennis shoes for their practice sessions so that they can develop sensitivity to the technique of "touching" the ball. Touching, or moving the ball with precision, is every bit as important as slamming it or kicking it with force. But if you do want to buy soccer shoes, choose a flexible pair with interchangeable cleats. There are several famous international brands that guarantee quality, such as Adidas and Puma.

Protectors. Soccer is a game where there shouldn't be any intentional physical contact, but it inevitably happens. I recommend the use of protectors, such as kneepads, front-leg pads, and gloves for the goalkeeper. The leg pads protect the front of the leg, especially the tibia or shinbone. Use the pads when practicing because the bones are most vulnerable in this part of the body. It is especially important for the goalie to be protected in this way because he is particularly susceptible to many falls. A small rock on the field can cause grave injury to him. The gloves will help protect the skin of his hands.

Let's start with the adult who may supervise and coach the game. Either you have experience in soccer or you don't. In either case I guarantee that you will have more fun if you follow some of the rules that will be mentioned here.

The Coach and the Child

Let's assume that you don't have much experience with the game yourself. Well, in the first place, don't worry about it. The most

9

important thing is your attitude — your enthusiasm to learn the game along with the children. Age is really of no importance and I don't intend for this to be a rigid system of training. These games can be fun for you as well as for the kids.

If you don't have any experience with the game of soccer, don't act as if you do. The kids will know it and you'll lose your authority. Be honest; it will make everything easier. Direct the group as a leader but don't be too rigid an organizer.

If you do have experience, remember that for the child the most important thing is the actual playing of the game and the most important thing for you is to help him learn how. There are three possible positions open to you as the coach:

1. Tell each player what to do.
2. Say nothing and just watch them play.
3. Discuss the techniques involved before playing. Then let them play and afterward discuss the techniques again.

Needless to say, the third position is the one by which the children will profit most and is the most desirable to assume. The games this book describes are all designed to achieve the technical and tactical aspects of soccer while they contribute to the physical strength of the players.

In order for each player to develop emotionally as well as physically, it's important to allow each person to think of possibilities for himself. This will help him in making decisions and in reaching his own conclusions about plays rather than merely following orders. This process may be slow and may involve a long evolution, so don't expect immediate results.

If you are a parent, one of the most difficult situations is coaching your own child. There are often underlying fears for him and reasons for wanting him to do especially well, as well as his own apprehensions. Consider these things if you are acting as the coach. Above all the playing of these game should be fun.

Soccer is Fun

Soccer can be great fun for children of almost all ages — even those who are very small and young. For those under fourteen years, it's important that they learn good technique that will help them when they are involved in more serious competition later. Eventually — as all good players do — they will develop their own personal ways of doing things and a personal technique will evolve.

To reach the point where a player has mastery over his technique is a long process in every sport (and in every art, for that matter). It requires much concentration. The point in question is how to motivate that concentration and discipline in very young children. In my experience I've found that the hardest thing is to force children to practice when they aren't having fun. If a child is having fun, on the other hand, he won't notice he is practicing.

Children learn by watching as well as by playing. So, if possible, provide pictures, films, demonstrations of successful game plays, and the opportunity to watch matches on television. These experiences will help the child see the proper movements and he will be able to memorize them without much effort.

It's very important for you as the coach to keep your patience while the children are learning; it is the only way that satisfactory results will be obtained.

To teach or to learn a specific technique follow these steps:

1. Visualize the correct movement. Watch it several times and think about it carefully.
2. Repeat the technique until the movement can be performed in an easy and relaxed manner.

It isn't important to explain this process to the children; children are interested in playing. It is important that you think about *him* and the best ways for him to learn. If you forget about him your efforts to teach him will be wasted. The games in this book have all been designed with the children in mind so that they can have fun with soccer techniques while they are learning the skills that will help them play the game.

One aspect of coaching that requires a great deal of tact is the technique of correcting technical errors. I recommend the following method:

1. Briefly describe the correct technique.
2. Demonstrate it.
3. Have the players practice it in a game play that uses it.
4. Discuss the technique and then answer questions that may come up about it.
5. Briefly explain the game that you have chosen to practice the technique.
6. Play the game. Praise all the players and encourage those players who seem to have skill in the technique to help those who haven't. Peer teaching, in many cases, is *more* effective than teaching by adults.

If you must correct or explain to a child a particular error, I highly recommend that you do it privately and with much discretion. The simulation of the technique and the practice of it is where learning takes place. Remember the successes of each player and believe in the ability of each individual to learn and to succeed. Try to give each player the desire to repeat the play a couple of times.

If you have had previous experience in soccer yourself it will be easy for you to follow the technical instructions and to observe them meticulously. Choose a game that is slightly difficult. It will be more beneficial for you and for the players to be challenged to learn it. If you don't have much experience, remember that it will come. And if you need some personal advice think of a neighbor or friend who is from Europe or Latin America; most of them will have played soccer as children.

There are courses available for people interested in soccer in the United States. I recommend that you contact the U.S. Youth Soccer Association (a division of the U.S. Soccer Federation), 350 Fifth Avenue, Suite 4010, New York, N.Y. 10001. This organization can inform you of activities in your locale and of leagues in your area. Or you can do as we did when I was growing up in Argentina: we organized neighborhood teams ourselves. And this informal method of training can't be such a bad idea because in 1978 Argentina won the World Cup.

When the child is ready to hit the ball and begin to play, explain the importance of good technique to him so that he can begin to practice it. Choose the games that will best practice the techniques that need work. Children will observe their fellow players and will try not to commit errors. You'll see that you won't actually have to coach much and that's really the whole point. Most places in the world children learn the fundamentals of the game without being supervised and learning from their peers.

When children practice daily the difference it will make will be amazing. You don't have to insist on technical perfection; professionals themselves are always improving their own techniques. Soccer should be played to be enjoyed — and before you know it every player will have improved.

All games have elements that eventually develop tactical problems that the participants must resolve. These should be resolved through discussion and the participation of all the playing members. Cooperation is of the utmost importance in this game and wisdom is gained throughout the experience of playing. The wisdom that is gained will then apply to all other parts of your life.

Soccer is a game in which imagination plays a very important part. To develop the creative aspect of the game you must allow the children the freedom to think for themselves and the liberty to develop their own individuality.

Sometimes teachers demand that their pupils gain control over technique before allowing them the freedom to express themselves, while some teachers believe that the freedom of expression is just as important as technique and should be learned right along with it. I think both technique and creativity are important to soccer. It has been said that the most effective way of teaching *anything* is through the medium of the game. In my opinion this is the *only* way to learn.

Chapter Two

BODY CONTROL

Control of the body requires time and dedication but it really isn't so difficult that everyone can't attain it. If you practice the games that are presented in this book you'll be surprised to find that in a very short time you will increase your strength, you'll become much more flexible in your back and limbs, and your general state of health — including your appetite — will be much improved. You will also have good physical endurance.

Before beginning any exercise I recommend warming up beforehand with a light trot or by jumping rope or by gently dribbling a ball. Exercise until you begin to perspire and then change to some stretching exercises. Now you're ready to play and you might want to try Juggling (see p. 80).

The most common error for a soccer player to make while he is exercising is to pretend that he is a track star. Many players make this mistake and ignore the fact that the objectives in playing soccer and running track are distinctly different.

How to Run

The track runner concentrates on speed and displays a rhythm in run, while the soccer player runs but is always thinking about what he is going to do with the ball. He must think about outwitting his opponent, eluding the defense, changing the rhythm or direction of his run.

Each soccer player will develop his own running technique and his own methods of moving. The speed of the game doesn't always depend on the speed of the individual player. Other activities, such as passing and receiving, are very important as well. If there is a delay in passing or if the recipient doesn't know what to do with the ball once he has it then the entire game will slow down.

If you play these games with pleasure, they will perfect your technique of running without your even thinking about it. Another good game for practicing running technique is The Slalom (see p. 72). Don't forget to note your timing in the different directions; this way you will appreciate the effort you put into the technique and see how it pays off. Practice the games with or without a ball — especially practice changing direction. Watch how professional soccer players in televised matches change direction and try to see how they can maintain their fast pace. This way you will begin to notice what you and your teammates can do to improve your speed.

How to Jump

Soccer requires all kinds of jumps and leaps. They differ in height and in length; they may be done with or without running; they may or may not require preparation. Sometimes you will jump by yourself or sometimes you will jump with another player when disputing the ball.

When practicing jumping alone, I recommend that you start with one foot and then jump with two feet. When you've mastered this technique, begin using the techniques that require using the head. One good one is The Pendulum (see p. 00).

Remember that you cannot lift your knee when you jump next to an opponent. This constitutes a foul even if you don't actually touch him. The games that you play incorporate different kinds of jumps and will give you the opportunity to improve your performance. Go to Chapter Four on the rules of the game and read over them. There are restrictions on the movement of your arms when you jump as well, although it may feel natural to you to move your arms. Your movements may be interpreted by the referee as an attempt to obstruct the jump being made by your opponent.

Jump with your arms close to your body and make sure that none of your opponents are near you. Practice your jumps with these ideas in mind but also remember that jumping in soccer is very much like jumping in any other sport. So *jump* — it's a magnificent sensation.

How To Build Endurance

The task of building resistance to fatigue has two steps: the first is a short period involving approximately two months; the second consists of periods of intense training.

For the first fifteen days of the initial period of training you will unquestionably feel that the training is very difficult. I would advise going at it lightly and progressing slowly. Endurance is built most effectively through prolonged periods of progressively harder labor: that is to say, you will gradually increase practice that uses more physical effort. Progress must be made little by little. Each week you can add three to five minutes more of training time or you can choose a different game that will require more strength and effort to perform. Maintain this gradual, strength-building pace and don't try to hurry the process. If your training schedule causes some fatigue, don't worry; always stop short before you reach the point of exhaustion. Try to practice at least three times a week to maintain the strength that you have built.

In completing the first step your body goes through an adaptation period that you should watch for and recognize. During this period your cardio-vascular system is changed in the following ways:

1. Your heart will be able to pump more blood.
2. There is a reduction in the palpitations of the heart.
3. Your heart, which is a muscle, will become stronger.
4. You will have better circulation of blood.

Rest and Nutrition. It you want to do a good job on the field, you should watch not only your hours in training, but the hours of rest that your body requires as well. You should get at least eight hours sleep every night.

Another important aspect of fitness is nutrition. You should make certain that your diet is rich in proteins, carbohydrates, vitamins, and minerals. It is especially important to maintain a balanced diet while your bones and muscles are still growing. A good rule to follow is to eat foods from the four main food groups each day:

1. Meat and eggs.
2. Raw and cooked vegetables and fresh fruit.
3. Bread and cereals.
4. Dairy products, such as milk and cheese.

Remember, too, that ideally you should eat four times a day — breakfast, lunch, a snack, and dinner. These meals should be separated by three to four hours. Eat and drink in moderation and try to develop good eating habits that will last for your entire lifetime. Your good diet will drastically affect your performance on the field.

In general, the foods that professional soccer players are told to avoid are heavy, greasy foods that are fried or heavily seasoned, and alcoholic beverages.

When you finish practice for the day, quench your thirst with water from the tap or cooler, or with mineral water. There are prepared drinks such as Gatorade that help restore the minerals that have been lost during practice and will cut your thirst as they revive you. Fruit juices are also good after practice.

You should try to eat at least three hours before practice to avoid feeling too full. Follow these simple rules for diet and you will notice that you'll tire less and feel much better.

Oh, and one more thing: stay completely away from JUNK food.

Chapter Three

TECHNIQUE

Everyone knows that in order to be a star in a sport it's important to have control over the techniques involved in playing the game. It would be ridiculous to think that one could learn the secrets of soccer by any system other than practice. Skill will come with experience.

I learned everything I know about soccer by playing it. In the days when I was growing up in Argentina we didn't have the benefit of coaches and there was certainly no talk about "total soccer" as there is today. We played soccer simply because we enjoyed it. It was practically the only game there was and we thought that the only way to enjoy an afternoon was to spend it with a soccer ball. I still believe that.

The moments of pleasure that the game has brought me are really what I'd like to convey to you. If you love this game you will learn to play it and to play it well. Leonardo da Vinci once said, "To learn is to love." Well, to love is to learn as well.

In Argentina when a player is planning to try out for a professional team it is because he is very certain that he is in control of his technique. The fascinating thing about this method is that up until that time he is completely self-taught and this will be his first encounter with a coach. People learn by playing; they don't need to have coaches explaining tactical systems such as "WM" or "4-3-3" to them for them to be fabulous players. These players in Argentina come to the team with the skills that allow them to control the ball and the players from Latin America are famous throughout the world for their precision in ball control. Uruguay has been world champion twice and Brazil has won the World Cup three times. Latin American countries have actually won the Cup more times than the countries in Europe where the game was invented. It is also interesting to note that European teams frequently bring Latin American players to Europe to play for them while the reverse very rarely happens.

Let's take a closer look at the two schools of thought and try to see how Latin American and European techniques differ. I'd like to begin by making an analogy between art and music and the game of soccer. The Europeans are Classicists in terms of their philosophy of the game. They rely upon a definite pattern for the game and the style of it is set by an agreement that the team is more important than the individual players. Because of this, there is little room for individuality on the field. Each player is part of a structure and that structure takes precedence over the individual player.

Latin Americans — on the other hand — play in a very different style. The player is freer and is not expected to fit rigidly into a structure. He is expected to participate with his teammates in the sporting event but he is also expected to play creatively. He is the Impressionist.

It is my opinion that soccer — like art and music — relies on creativity. The reason that the Latin American teams do so well in worldwide competition is that they are encouraged to play the game creatively.

This is not to say that a team should be composed of eleven individuals, each doing his own thing without regard for his teammates. It's important to try to find a balance between the Classical and Impressionistic approaches — between the individual and the team as a whole.

A good soccer player should be in total control of the ball. How can he achieve this? Simply by practicing. Repetition of the drills over a long period of time may at first seem discouraging and boring. But if you use the drills to have fun you will find you are entertained at the same time you are practicing the drills.

If you are coaching, watch to see which players need special help with certain drills. You may want to coach them individually. If you are a player and know you need help with a certain technique, you might ask one of your teammates to give you some advice. Your team will be strengthened if you all learn to help one another.

Before you begin to play you will need to understand the following terms:

This is one of the most technical elements in the game of soccer. There are various ways to kick that use different parts of the foot: *Instep.* The part that goes from the toes to the foot up to the ankle is the instep of your foot. This part is used to kick the ball no matter what your position or your height. The instep is used to kick the ball so that you can obtain a shot of good power and direction. (See Fig. 3.1). The moment that you shoot you put your left foot alongside the

Kicking

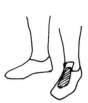

ball. The right foot goes back while the toes curl to create an arch in the instep. Direct the right foot at the ball and kick it with such impact as to place it as high as you want in the pass. If you hit below the center of the ball the ball will go too high. If you hit it in the center, it will barely skim above the ground.

Outside foot. This is the part of the foot that goes from the toes to the ankle on the exterior side of the foot (see Fig. 3.2). You will appreciate this kick as you practice it because it involves a touch that is very difficult to achieve. For this reason, it is difficult to gain any power with this kick but it is especially useful for short passes that need great speed. Very little body movement is necessary. Through its use, it is possible to give the ball purpose and because of the shape of the arc it makes it is sometimes called the "banana shot."

Inside foot. I have deliberately left this touch for last. It is the most sure way of executing short passes or passes of medium distance. You will use this kick in almost all the games that this book contains. It can be a short, forceful kick, or a long, deliberate swing from the hip. In the short kick you turn the ball against the foot — in the long kick you almost push the ball towards the desired direction with the leg following in that direction. To do both these kicks, you use the interior of the foot that goes from the big toe to the ankle bone (see Fig. 3.3). Practice this touch with all the exercises; it's the best way to learn. Once it seems easy to use this technique, work at it with the instep. When you've mastered that, work with the exterior of the foot.

Finally, I recommend that you observe how the professionals use this touch by seeing films or by watching matches on television. Once you become accustomed to seeing it, invite someone to join you and practice this touch with him.

Basically, these are the three touches that you should master. Then you can practice with the heel, the knee, and, if you wish, the point of the foot by using the toes. But at the beginning don't attempt too much. Try to practice the kick with the interior of the foot and the instep kick carefully. You can play well with these two touches alone.

Trapping

Trapping means bringing the ball under your control by using the feet, the body or the head. It is every bit as important to know how to receive the ball as it is to know how to pass it.

The ball will arrive in various manners. It may be a little off the ground; it may be high up; it may be fast or slow. For each of these balls you must respond with the correct trapping technique.

To receive the ball we use the foot, the leg, the chest, and the head. Every part of the body may be used except for the arms and

hands. (See Fig. 3.4). Whichever of these methods you use, the same principle applies: Avoid letting the ball rebound away from you. Produce a yielding movement that lessens the ball's force on impact and breaks the ball's movement away from you. To receive the ball with the foot or the leg the muscles should be relaxed. Work with the ball to find out the different ways to lessen the ball's force.

The leg. The thigh is used often to trap balls that come at you at medium elevation. The muscle mass forms a spacious surface for trapping and its smoothness will also help lessen the impact. Relax the thigh by giving way with the ball; you'll reduce the possibility of rebounding it from the leg.

The chest. Receiving the ball with the chest requires bending of the knees and holding the chest relaxed with a slight backward tilt. The arms and shoulders should move forward at the moment of impact.

The head. Last of all, we can receive the ball with the head. Actually, the part of the head that the ball strikes is the forehead when the body is relaxed. The knees should be bent and, at the moment of impact, the body should move slightly backward. The movement enables the ball to rebound slightly and fall at your feet. You then can continue on the field with it in your control. It's important to remember not to close your eyes when head trapping.

Dribbling

Dribbling is the most effective resource a player has in the attack. Closed defense teams of nine men aren't much use against a person like Pele who is able to elude three or four men at the same time. Dribbling is the most important ability that the forward can possess. This technique is incorporated into many of the games at the back of this book and is stressed for this reason.

Dribbling becomes extremely important as a tool to use against the defense — specifically to catch the defense and to keep them off their guard. When a forward eludes two or three men it is certain that there are one or two unmarked (or unguarded) teammates on the field. That is the time when a pass can be made. The good dribblers focus their attention on the defense and if they get the chance to enter their opponent's area without a guard on them they have a greater opportunity to make a goal.

It's good for the beginner to make certain he practices all the games that demand controlling the ball with both legs. Both variations of The Labyrinth (Games 15 and 16) and The Cooperation Relay (Game 22) involve this skill. Practice consistently for a short period of time and when you are in a real game you will discover that the natural dispute over the ball will teach you the rest. The main thing is to learn to control the ball — changing legs, changing direction, and changing speed — then learning to protect the ball. The next step is to keep it away from opponents and finally you must learn to pass it.

There are many ways of dribbling. The fascinating thing about it is that you can often understand the personality of a player by the way he dribbles: his aggression or anger will show. The player will develop a form that best suits his style — and a player's style very often depends upon his mental and emotional maturity.

In the beginning it is difficult and frustrating when someone makes fun of you, but this is always a moment when learning can take place. Ignore what he is saying and observe the body of your opponent. Pay attention to his movements and the distance from which he places himself from the ball. (When it is close to him, for example, it will be difficult or impossible for you to get at it.) Observe the steps that he takes and you will see that they are short and powerful. When he escapes from you, his steps will lengthen. Don't feel disappointed: no one is born with perseverance; it must be learned.

The ball is your friend and will surely give you lots of pleasure. Each time you hit it, do it carefully. Concentrate on what you are going to do before you do it.

Throwing-In

This launching technique is very easy and doesn't require any special commentary by me. See the chapter on the rules of the game for the times when throwing-in is necessary.

Passing

Passing the ball is nothing more than just a normal occurrence in the development of the game. The pass implies an emotional maturity on the part of the passer because he must overcome the temptation to "possess" the ball and to not give it away. This maturity is something that is difficult for even professional players to achieve. In soccer it is very important to believe in others. To pass the ball you must believe in your teammates just as much as you believe in yourself. Many people make the mistake of keeping the ball to themselves and they make excuses to themselves about why they haven't passed it. The real reason is that they feel that their teammates cannot move the ball as well as they can themselves.

Children especially must learn to share the field. Everyone is interested in making a goal. The emphasis in the game should be on achieving the goal through cooperation and maneuvering the ball by many people on the field. The game of soccer is fundamentally a game of working together as a team. In soccer everyone — even the goalkeeper — is a quarterback. The goalkeeper can make a pass good enough to work towards a triumphant goal.

Be generous. Pass the ball rapidly. If everyone has this attitude the whole team will benefit.

The goalkeeper is the last man on the defense and is the only one on the team who can touch the ball with his hands. It is a position of great responsibility; his errors usually result in a goal for his opponents.

Goalkeeping

Children often would rather not play this position because it usually is a long time between contacts with the ball. Because the goalkeeper must use his hands, people who have had some experience in playing basketball have a considerable advantage in playing this position. They know how to receive, to throw and to control the ball when it comes high in the air. A good point to remember when playing is that no player can charge at the goalie.

The most interesting aspect of the position of goalie is his "diving," or jumping for the ball. There is nothing more spectacular to watch than this natural intervention. To learn how to do this I recommend working on a smooth surface — either a good lawn or another smooth surface. Make sure to wear protective pads for your knees and wear gloves on your hands. Many of the games in this book have positions for the goalie.

It is also important to remember that as goalie you also need to know how to kick, dribble and throw powerfully.

Chapter Four
A SHORT COURSE IN THE RULES

Soccer is played in more than 140 countries throughout the world. All soccer-playing countries belong to an organization called the Federation of International Football Associations. The FIFA sets the rules of the game for international competitions and organizes international tournaments. The World Cup Tournament is held every four years — alternating in setting between the Americas and Europe. The last one was held in 1978 in Argentina; the next will be held in Spain in 1982.

The rules of the game are strictly observed in all the countries that belong to the association. It isn't necessary that you, as a soccer player, know every detail of the rules, but, in order to play, you and your friends should have at least an idea about errors and penalties.

The Field

In the games I have used various dimensions on fields to suit the needs of the different plays. These dimensions are noted but it's a good idea to know that a regulation field should measure 50 to 100 yards in width and 100 to 130 yards in length. Prepare yourself for a lot of running.

The Ball

The ball should be round and made of leather or of any other material that the FIFA has authorized. It should measure between 27 and 28 inches in circumference and weigh between 14 and 16 ounces. The referee is the only person who is authorized to determine whether or not the ball is within regulations.

Number of Players

In regulation soccer there are eleven players and each league decides how many changes can be made during the course of the game. In international competition the number of changes is limited to three substitutions.

Uniforms for Players

A player cannot wear objects such as watches or rings or other shapr instruments onto the field that might be dangerous to himself or to the other players. The goalkeeper should wear a different-colored shirt so that he is distinguished from the other players. The players should each wear a number on their backs starting with the number 1 for the goalie and ascending to the number 11 for the left wing. The numbers should be large and visible like the ones that football players wear.

The referee is the only authority on the field. His decisions are absolutely final. He can expel any player in the game by giving him a red card. He doesn't necessarily have to warn that player by giving him a yellow card before this expulsion. He will expel without warning if he feels that the rules have been violated intentionally. Another duty of the referee is to be aware of the minutes in a game and to make sure that the players are dressed according to regulation. He is basically responsible for the ebb and the flow of the game. His uniform is black — the color reserved for him. No team may use black as the color of its shirts.

The Referee

Two linesmen are used to assist the referee. Their duties consist of calling offsides or indicating whether the kick was a corner kick. (They also point out when the ball completely crosses the touchline.) The linesmen assist the referee by watching the time and by observing goal kicks or fouls that the referee cannot see because of the position he may be in. They usually wear yellow or red flags.

The Side Referee

Soccer is played in two 45-minute periods with a total playing time of 90 minutes. At the end of the first half there is a 5- to 15-minute break. In the games I offer in this book I suggest the following time periods:

    Ages 6 to 9: two halves of 30 minutes each.
    Ages 9 to 12: two halves of 40 minutes each.
    Ages 12 and over: two halves of 45 minutes each.

    No one knows better than you do when your body has had enough. Don't try to force yourself when you feel tired. If you're just beginning at soccer, start gradually. Soccer demands great physical effort. You should develop strength over a long period of time, building your endurance progressively.

Duration of the Game

To decide who starts the game, a coin is tossed; the winner of the toss starts the first half and the loser starts the second half. When a team makes a goal the game is restarted in the center of the field by the opposite team.

    In the second half of the game the teams change places or goals. When the game is stopped for any reason other than an infringement of the rules (if, for example, a player is injured) then the game is restarted with a drop kick. This consists of making the ball fall in front of the players who then scramble for it. Another situation that would demand that the game be restarted is if the ball went flat

The Start of the Game (The Kickoff)

during the game and needed to be replaced. Still another situation would be if the posts or the net were damaged and time out had to be called, or if animals or people came out on the field and the game had to be halted and then restarted.

When the Ball Is in and Out of Play

The ball is out of play when it has completely crossed the border lines of the field, or has totally crossed the goal lines (either the touchline or the goal line), and when the referee interrupts the game. If the ball rebounds on the posts, crossbars, or any of the corner flags, it is still in play. The same is true if the ball rebounds from the body of the referee.

The players cannot decide for themselves when to hold up the game; the referee is the only one who can do this. If a player from Team A sends the ball across his own goal line, Team B is entitled to a corner kick.

Scoring

A goal is scored when the ball totally passes the goal line going between the posts and the crossbar. The team scoring the MOST goals is the winner. In the case of neither team scoring or if there is a tie between the two teams, the goal is not legal when scored in the following ways:

1. Indirect free kick (made by passing to a teammate who scores)
2. Goal kick
3. Kickoff
4. Drop kick
5. Throw-in

You may complete a direct goal in the following situations:

1. Direct free kick
2. Corner kick
3. Penalty kick

You may also complete a direct goal in whatever manner is natural in the action. A goal is valid if, by chance, a player mistakenly kicks successfully into his opponent's goal.

Offside

A player is in an offside position if — while the ball is being passed to him by his teammates — there are not at least two opponents between himself and the goal. But if he receives the ball in a throw-in, drop kick, corner kick, or by means of a goal kick, it is passed. The penalty for an offside offense is an indirect free kick for the opposite team. It is executed from the point on the field where the infraction occured.

Prohibited Acts

The rules penalize a team with a direct free kick to the opponents in the following violations:

1. A kick or an intent to kick an opponent.

2. Tripping an opponent with the foot or body.
3. Jumping over an opponent.
4. Charging an opponent violently or dangerously.
5. Charging an opponent from behind.
6. Striking or intending to strike an opponent.
7. Holding an opponent.
8. Pushing an opponent with the hands or arms.
9. Taking, bumping, or throwing the ball with the hands or arms. (The only exception to this last rule is that the goalie can touch the ball with his arms and hands in any manner.)

If any of these violations occurred in your penalty area the opponents have a penalty free kick.

Penalty

The free kick is executed from a distance of twelve yards, measured from the goal line to the ball. All the players, with the exception of the goalkeeper and the player kicking, must be outside the penalty area. The goalkeeper cannot move away from the goal line in any direction until the ball is kicked.

Throw-Ins

If the ball completely passes the lateral line (the touch line) there must be a throw-in. The throw-in is awarded to the team that did not touch the ball last. The player who execute the throw-in must observe certain details:
1. He should face the field.
2. He can only step on the lateral line (the touchline) with one foot.
3. He should have a part of each foot on the ground.
4. The ball must be thrown over the head with both hands.
5. He can enter the field without authorization from the referee.
6. The ball cannot be touched by the thrower until another player does. If he does, an indirect free kick is granted to the opposing team.
7. He cannot make a goal with the throw-in.

If the throw-in is not performed in accordance with the above rules, the opposite team is granted a throw-in.

Goal Kick

When the ball passes over the goal line directed by a player from the opposing team, the game is started again with the goal kick. The ball is placed at the point nearest the half where the ball went out of bounds. If the ball does not go out of the area, no one can touch it and the kick must be done over again. Any player can execute this kick, including the goalkeeper.

Corner Kick

If the ball is passed outside, over the goal line, by the defense, a corner kick is performed by the opposite team. It is executed with the foot from the corner of the side where the ball passed. A direct goal is valid and may be scored. The defensive team may form a barricade ten yards away from where the free or indirect kick is executed.

I suppose that after reading the summary of the rules of the game you will think that all of this is very complicated and difficult to remember. Well, I don't blame you because it took me many years to learn all these details. Don't be surprised if a referee tells you that all of these details are very interesting but that very few people know them. I have personally dedicated quite a bit of time to learning the "law" of the game, and, in doing so, have observed that many times one can make an error in judgment or in the interpretation of a point. Knowing that the decision of the referee is final and is without appeal, I feel it's a good personal rule to never discuss the game with the referee before, during, or after the game. The referees proceed in good faith and with honesty. Many times our emotions cloud things and let us see things only partially. Forget about the referee, go by his decision, and concentrate your energies on the game. Leave discussion for the next day when you're a bit more calm.

As you will see, there is often a controversy. A good philosophy to adopt is to always take things with humor. You and I aren't yet playing for the World Cup, right?

Compete joyously. If something comes out wrong then give it another try. Smile, and try to remember how marvelous it is to have another opportunity to try to make things turn out differently.

I play soccer every Saturday with a group of people on a field on the campus of a university near my house. The group is of such variety. There are young students from all over — Spain, Greece, Nigeria, Mexico, Canada, Japan. To be sure we all have different appreciations of the game and we avidly discuss each one. One of them — my friend Demetrios, who is from Greece — speaks wisdom when we have a dispute and he says, *"No internacionale."* None of us knows if he is speaking Italian, Greek or Spanish but I assure you, we all understand. Demetrios means that our game is not of international importance so there's no reason why we should play it as if it were. When he speaks, smiles light up and we continue the game.

Compete for enjoyment and you will see that these games will benefit your mental and physical health. When you feel just terrible because you just committed an error, do as my friend does and say to yourself, *"No internacionale."*

The best book on rules is *FAIR OR FOUL* by Paul and Larry Harrys. It was adopted as the official referees' manual because it is so complete.

50
games
with a
soccer ball.....

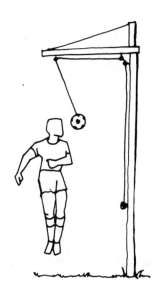

THE WALL

The simplicity of this game makes it ideal for the beginner. To begin playing, two people face one another forming The Wall (See Fig. 1). If you are just beginning to

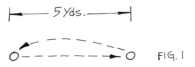

FIG. 1

play then you should be about 2 or 3 yards apart; if you're more advanced then 4 to 8 yards is a good distance.

If you are just beginning to play soccer, don't worry about following the rules strictly. As you improve, you can make the game more difficult by adhering to the rules. The rules can be varied in two ways:

1. Change the number of touches — the objective being to control the ball by passing and receiving.
2. Change the kind of kick to be used — the objective being to perfect the high kick and the medium-high kick using either the interior or the exterior of the foot.

With the two kicks you can practice receiving with the interior of the right foot and passing with the interior of the left foot. With one kick you can practice passing and receiving with the interior of the left foot. And for fun you can practice an unlimited number of kicks passing and receiving medium-high balls in the air or play with a partner.

Another variation is for the players to face in one direction. You can use the perimeter of the field, as shown in Figure 2, or a circular formation, as in Figure 3.

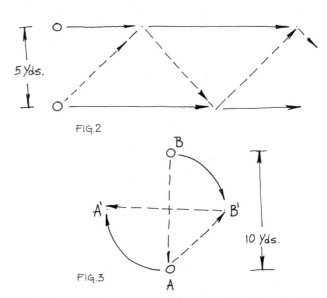

FIG.2

FIG.3

The most common mistakes in playing this game are flinging the ball outside the range of the other pass or passing the ball indirectly to the other player. Another mistake is to exceed the number of kicks originally agreed upon in passing, or to pass with a type of kick that wasn't agreed upon, or to make a variation in the height of the agreed-upon pass. All of these are common errors and don't be worried if you make them since this game is designed to teach you ball control.

THE
BRAID

This game is played in groups of three. It requires skill in technique, the feeling for space, and the knowledge of how to change speeds and when to execute a pass. In using this game, your peripheral vision (the ability to see to the side while looking ahead) is developed. Peripheral vision is very important in soccer.

In Figure 4, you can see the placement of the three participants and the direction that they are going. The passes are forward directed and the player needs to calculate the distance of the pass, the strength of the pass, and the speed of the return pass. This game is effectively played to the rear of the playing field.

The most common errors made while playing The Braid are:

1. Mistakes in the direction of the pass.
2. Mistakes in the type of the kick.
3. Mistakes in the height of the pass.
4. Mistakes in the number of kicks used to pass.

A variation of this game is to place four participants in what is called The Braid of H. There are two variations of The Braid of H, as you can see in Figure 5. One of them is that in the passing of the ball there is freedom to pass it to any man, while all the men continue to run in the same direction. The other variation is that passing may be done in an X formation only — the passes are vertical, horizontal, and diagonal (see Fig. 6).

I recommend that the players change positions after awhile. You can vary the number of kicks, the height and length of the passes and the kicks to add variety to the game. The ideal to strive for — although it takes much experience — is to complete each pass with only one touch of the ball. Good luck!

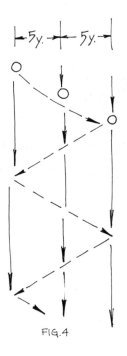

FIG. 4

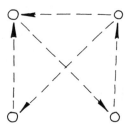

FIG. 5

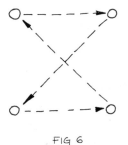

FIG 6

THE ZIGZAG

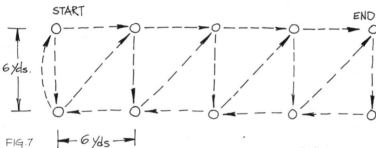

FIG.7

This game is perfect for you to practice your touches. The positions are stationary and this helps the player to concentrate on the technical aspects of kicking the ball. The winning team completes the pattern first.

The formation for this game is two parallel lines. In each line are four to six players facing one another and standing in one place, as in Figure 7.

I recommend that you go over the rules completely before you start to play this game in order to avoid confusion. As in all the games in this book, you can change the distance between players to suit your abilities. If you have two teams playing, I suggest that you use the formation shown in Figure 8. I've marked the position of the coach in the drawing so that he can serve as referee.

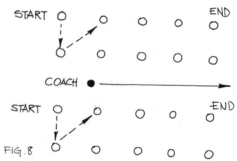

FIG.8

In case you don't have enough players to form a team, you can play this game with a few individuals and keep score by counting the errors each player makes. The player with the least number of errors is the winner.

Errors consist of passing the ball in the wrong direction, and exceeding the number of technical errors such as height of the ball, type of kick, or the number of kicks, which should all be determined by the skill of the players in your group.

BOWLING

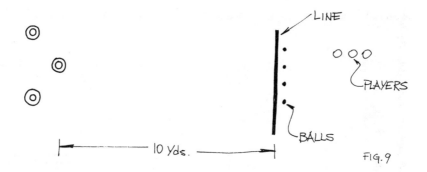

FIG. 9

Most of us have played this game — it consists of knocking down a set of pins from a certain distance away by using a ball. In soccer the objects that are knocked down are cones that are twice the size and weight of bowling pins. The distance that the players stand from the cones should be determined by the age and ability of the players.

To begin, align the cones as Figure 9 shows. In general, the distance between cones should be 1 yard with 8 yards or more between the cones and the players. Mark the boundary line on the ground. Now you are ready to play.

To make the game more interesting you can give a value in points to each cone and then add up the score at the end of the game. (See Fig. 10). The player with the highest score is the winner.

If you don't have a lot of experience, it's enough just to touch the cones with the ball — you don't have to knock them over. Later on you should try to knock them down in order to win the point. This will require major shooting power.

There are two ways to play this game. The first is for each person to shoot continuously (one shot after another) and to total his points for the round. The second is for each player to take turns shooting and then total the points. This game is lots of fun and everyone seems to love it.

You should be aware that the use of the legs, especially the left one, and the practicing of the different touches are the important parts of this game to practice. This can be achieved by:

1. Kicking with the right foot instep.
2. Kicking with the left foot instep.
3. Kicking with the outside of the right foot, and so forth.

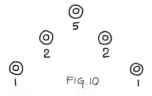

FIG. 10

THE WHEEL

This game not only improves the technique of passing, but is good for building endurance. To begin playing, the players form a circle with equal distance between them, as shown in Figure 11. The game consists of passing the ball to the player in the center who immediately returns it to the player next to him.

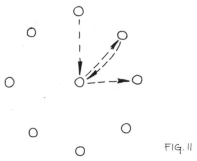

FIG. 11

After you have played it for awhile in this fashion, you can play with these variations:

1. The center player passes the ball counterclockwise, so that you use the opposite side of the foot or the opposite foot.

2. The players pass to the center player while they are running around the circle.

3. The center player passes the ball — skipping every other player — while all players are running around the circle. For this variation it's important to have an uneven number of players, as in Figure 12, so that everybody gets a turn. This game is particularly good after you've been

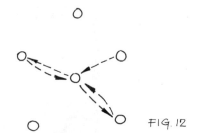

FIG. 12

playing soccer for awhile because you need to have greater control over the ball when you are running faster.

4. Have someone blow the whistle to keep changing the direction of the running. In addition, when the whistle blows use the opposite foot or a different kick.

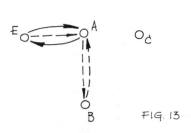

FIG. 13

Another interesting variation is for the player to run to a different station after having kicked the ball to that place. This will seem almost as if you are running to meet the ball. (See Fig. 13.) To begin this game, E passes the ball to A — E runs to the center while A, who has passed the ball to B, runs to E's place, and so forth. It is important that the field is clearly marked.

RANDOM
SHOOTING

6

This is a game of survival. Balls are coming from all directions and saving yourself is the only thing that you should think about. It is a game that educates your reflexes little by little. Your objective is to try to avoid being touched by a ball.

I suggest that you use a medicine ball or a ball that is sewn and stuffed with cloth. It must be a soft ball that won't hurt a player who might be surprised by the impact of it. This ball must only be kicked at the low level.

Mark the field clearly using three areas with a neutral zone between, as shown in Figure 14. The field can be as wide as you want it to be.

This game is played at first with only one ball. Each team should remain in its own area. Any player who is touched by the ball while it is being passed back and forth must leave the field. The team that eliminates the most players from the opposite side is the winner. In its variations this game becomes increasingly difficult:

1. At the start of the game each player has a ball.
2. The player who is touched then crosses the neutral zone and plays for the other team.
3. You can make restrictions in the in the use of different touches.
4. The ball is flung by hand and the players must be touched in the legs to be eliminated. (This is an especially good variation for small children.)

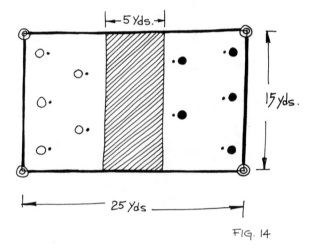

FIG. 14

THE CLEANUP

7

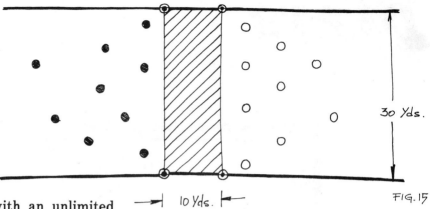

30 Yds.

10 Yds.

FIG. 15

There are two teams with an unlimited number of players on each team. (It would be best to use a large playing field for this game — you will do a lot of running that will build endurance.) Divide the field into three zones — one is neutral with no limitations on the width of it. A soccer field is appropriate because boundary lines are already marked (See Fig. 15.)

To begin the game each player has a ball that he flings to the opposite side of the field. The balls go back and forth continually and without stopping until one team has no balls in its area. This is very hard to do because balls are being kicked continuously — but it can be done. At that moment that team is declared the winner. Variations to this game include:

1. Placing a tennis net between the two playing areas for avoiding hard or powerful kicks.
2. Restrictions in the kick forms or the number of touches may be made.
3. You may also make restrictions in the number of passes.

When a player throws the ball out of bounds, the referee gives the opposing team a ball. The player to receive the ball from the referee passes first to the player nearest to him and that player flings it to the opposite field.

DARTS

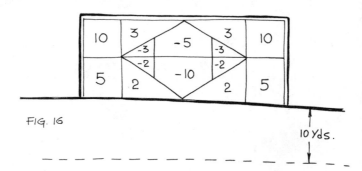

FIG. 16

10 Yds.

The continual practice of this game guarantees skillful execution of free kicks. In fact, this is the best way I know of to improve your kicking. Darts can be played in teams or individually. The game requires a wall where a goal area can be chalked or painted on.

The goal is divided into zones, as in Figure 16. These are given different values — either positive or negative. From a distance of 10 yards or more mark a boundary over which the players cannot cross. After determining the teams, begin the game with individual kicks. The score is kept either by the coach or by a scorekeeper that you agree upon.

As you can see in the illustration, the most vulnerable zones for the goalie protecting that area are those of high value. The central zones that have a negative value are ultimately subtracted from the total score. The central zone is where the goalie is situated; that area is given more protection. We want to learn to shoot outside the area that is well protected.

When everyone has acquired a certain degree of skill, you can move the line further away. Another variation consists of kicking the ball from outside the penalty area into the goal. In this variation the players learn to become more accurate in kicking from distant positions (see Fig. 17).

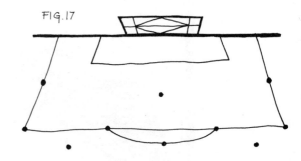

FIG. 17

Other variations include:
1. Changing legs.
2. Using different kicks.
3. Shooting from different distances.
4. Having a goalkeeper to protect the goal.

THE TURTLES

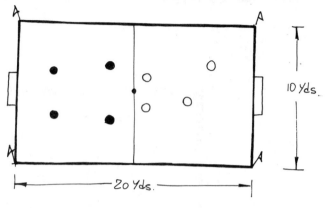

FIG. 18

This is really an enjoyable game played in groups of eight with four on each team. Smooth surfaces such as lawn, dirt, or beach should be used. This game is especially suited to train players in quick reaction and recovery from a fall. The more difficult the playing surface (such as beach sand, which is soft and uneven), the stronger the player's muscles will become. In a real game he will find it much easier to get up and get going after a spill.

This game benefits the arms, the torso, and the legs, which receive a total workout — something they are most unaccustomed to. This is a game to strengthen physical endurance.

If you play in a limited space, the players must observe the same rules that are used in a common match except that they play in a position where the hands and knees are touching the floor, face down. The players go forward and backward like turtles. A medicine ball is used. It is prohibited to move the ball off the ground and you may only use your hands to move the ball. The object is to put the ball in the goal. The winning team is the one that makes the most number of goals in two periods of play. Each period should be 10 minutes in length with a 5-minute break between.

In this game dribbling with one hand only is permitted. Holding the ball with both hands is not. This error is penalized with a free throw for the other team.

When the ball goes out of bounds laterally (along the length of the playing area) it is put into play again with a throw-in using both arms. When the ball goes out of bounds on the goal lines sides, a corner kick (with the hands) is used to put the ball into play. Those are the only two circumstances in which the ball can be passed through the air.

A goal occurring from a lateral throw-in or from a corner kick is not valid.

There is a tendency in this game to "walk" with the knees. When a player commits this error, a direct free kick is taken in that position and if the same player is penalized three times for the same error he must leave the game and cannot be replaced.

The variations to this game are to change the type of ball by using a light regulation soccer ball.

BOMBARDMENT

In this game the power of the shot (the players' ability to pass the ball a long distance) is emphasized. The objective is for each team to clear its playing area of the oncoming ball or balls. The playing area should be about the size of a soccer field but you can make the size of the field smaller if it suits your team better. This playing area should be divided into three areas, as in Figure 19. The middle area is a

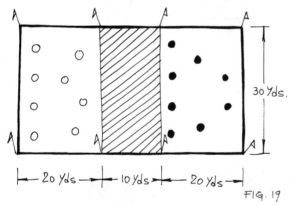

30 Yds.

|— 20 Yds —|— 10 Yds —|— 20 Yds —|

FIG. 19

neutral area and the area on the ends of it is where each team is placed. The teams can move around freely in their own areas but they cannot enter the middle or neutral area. The number of players can be adapted to the available space and to the technical skills of the players.

This game can be played with one or two balls and a point is made when the ball goes over the opponent's touchline, as shown in the illustration. When the ball goes out of bounds it is put into play again by a throw-in. If an error is committed in the throwing of the ball, the other team gets a throw-in from any side of its field. The important thing to practice here is the kick and the variations are as follows:

1. Changing legs.
2. Change the kind of touch.
3. Change the number of touches you can have in your area.
4. Vary the number and kind of balls used.
5. Restrict the number of touches that each player is allowed.

I recommend that in the beginning you play with only one ball and that three passes are allowed in each area. It is best if you start with a maximum of three touches allowed to each player. As you become more skillful you can reduce the number of passes as well. In doing this it becomes more difficult to clear the balls from an area. Points are easily lost and, in general, the players will have to work harder to try to win the game.

THE CRABS

This game is played in a sitting-down position. It sounds easy but it is a very demanding way to play. The game helps to strengthen the arms and particularly the muscles in your abdomen. It is also a funny game because of the positions you find yourself in.

For this game a medicine ball is used and it must only be rolled on the floor, as in Figure 20. To advance forward or to go backward you can move your body but can-

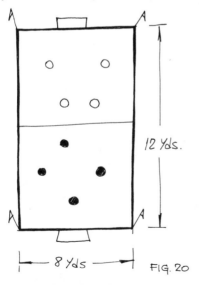

12 Yds.

8 Yds.   FIG. 20

not abandon your sitting-down position. This makes moving the ball rather difficult. It's best to use your space by playing four against four as this allows good circulation of the ball and constant movement of the players. Play in two periods of 10 minutes each with a 3-minute break between them. The game is most fun when you play on natural grass or on sand.

If the ball goes out of bounds or over the goal line, a throw-in using both hands from a kneeling position is used to put the ball back in play. The throw-in occurs from the point at which the ball went out of bounds or from the corner.

The use of the foot is penalized with a free kick. To play in any position except the sitting-down one is penalized with a free kick. Dribbling is permitted but holding the ball with both hands is prohibited and penalized with a free throw-in for the opposing team. Variations of this game include:

1. The use of light balls such as a soccer ball or a tennis ball.
2. The use of a football.
3. Using both the feet and the hands to play.

49

THE DUCK THROW

In this game the emphasis is on the accuracy of each player's aim. The game consists of sending the duck (the ball) to the opponent's side of the field and trying to avoid its return to your side.

In a limited playing space, you place two teams separated by a neutral area which we refer to as the lake. You place the duck (the medicine ball) in the lake and then you go hunting for it by trying to hit it with your soccer ball. You try to find a home for the duck, hopefully in your opponent's playing area, as you can see in Figure 21.

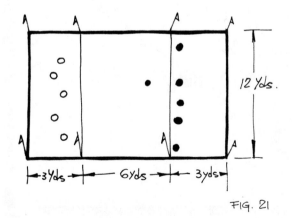

FIG. 21

You can play with one or with several balls. If you use several there are more opportunities for participation even though the possibility of making the game confusing exists. Your attempt to hunt the duck will be successful only if your shot is accurate and well aimed. The shot must be precise and powerful because the medicine ball is heavier than the balls that you will be throwing at it.

While the players are hunting (using their balls to hit the medicine ball) they must be constantly searching for another ball. This is done by taking the balls that have come onto the playing area from their opponent's side. It seems simple enough but it does add another dimension. This will improve your ability to think and react quickly.

One variation of this game consists of giving each player a turn at shooting. This makes the game move more slowly; each player has his own ball and takes his chance at hunting the duck and alternating in attack and defense. The team which has forced the duck to the opposite field the most times is the winner.

THE
DOOR

This is an ideal game for the technical and tactical benefits that it affords you. In the technical aspect, you should concentrate on learning to continually keep your eye on the ball. The tactical aspect is that you must learn to return the ball with precision and accuracy. (See Fig. 22.)

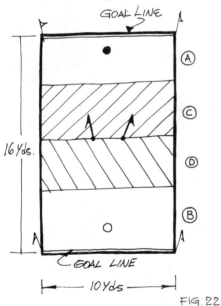

FIG. 22

To mark the field use stakes and lines. The area should not be too large because you will be playing one to one or two to two. The field is divided into four equal zones. Zones A and B are for the players; zones C and D are neutral areas that are not occupied by anyone. If the ball is thrown offside (out of bounds), the opposite team gets a direct throw-in. The object of the game is to pass the ball between flags that we call "the door" to the goal line. When the ball goes over the goal line that team wins a point.

If the players have some experience in the technique of kicking you can eliminate the neutral zone or enlarge it and reduce the width of the door. If a ball is thrown out to the side or it doesn't pass through the door by Team A then Team B gets an outside throw-in from its own goal line. The same is true when the ball enters the neutral zone.

Generally the game is played with one or two touches, but if the game is played with pairs of players, you can add one or two passes. This makes the game more interesting and fast moving.

There are two periods of play which are 10 minutes each with a 5-minute break between them. Or if you like you can set goal limits instead of a time limit. There might be a limit of ten goals for each, with the teams changing sides after the first five goals. The first team to achieve ten goals is the winner.

To make the game more difficult, you can make restrictions such as allowing the use of only one leg or changing the kick after a certain amount of time has elapsed.

THE CAN

One of the biggest problems coaches have all over the world is getting the players to put the balls back when they've finished their practice. Thinking of this, I remembered a teacher of mine who devised a game that I played when I was an amateur. When we finished practice we had to kick the balls into an old can that the coach placed on the lawn for us. Whoever was successful at making the shot got to go to the showers. This was fun for all except the poor soul who was last and who had to carry all the balls back to the equipment room. Obviously, no one wanted to be last. We practiced this exercise every day, sometimes even at home.

This game is played in a circular formation. The players stand outside of the circle. A big barrel — or three or four tires stacked on top of one another — is placed in the middle of the circle. The players then attempt to put the ball into the barrel.

This game can be played individually or in teams. And don't be fooled by its seeming simplicity; it isn't all that easy to score a point. However, if you do know how to use your feet properly you can double your number of successfully executed shots.

The interior instep is commonly used to make this shot. You can also use the end of the instep (the toes of the foot). Place your toes as close as possible to the point where the ball rests, as shown in Figure 23.

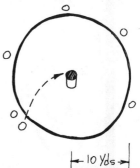

Then with a quick movement, lift the leg in the direction of the object. The ball is practically resting in the "spoon" that the arch forms and can easily be sent in the right direction. Be sure to practice this. When everyone is skillful enough at doing this, you can vary the game by using a different kick to make the goal.

THE LABYRINTH I

The most important technical aspect of this game is that the player learns to control the ball while dribbling. He must control the ball close to the foot while constantly changing directions. This gives him speed, builds his endurance, and helps him develop tenacity. Controlling the ball while dribbling is difficult because there is always an opponent close by who is ready to take the ball away.

The best way to begin this game is for the players to arrange themselves in a line formation. There should be a line of about twenty cones and another line of twenty chairs. The players begin by passing the ball around the cones. There should be an interval of 10 seconds between players; this will help eliminate obstructions later on down the line. The next thing they do is to pass the ball through the legs of the chair. After that they pass the ball over the back of the chair and the last thing that they do is shoot the ball to a wall, rebound it, and then pass the ball to the next one in

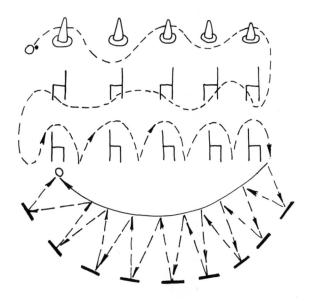

the line. Meanwhile the player who finishes The Labyrinth gets in line again.

This game can be played individually or in teams. Scoring is achieved by keeping track of the time or by keeping track of the errors. Variations can be made in the kicks, the speed, or in a combination of both.

THE
LABYRINTH II

16

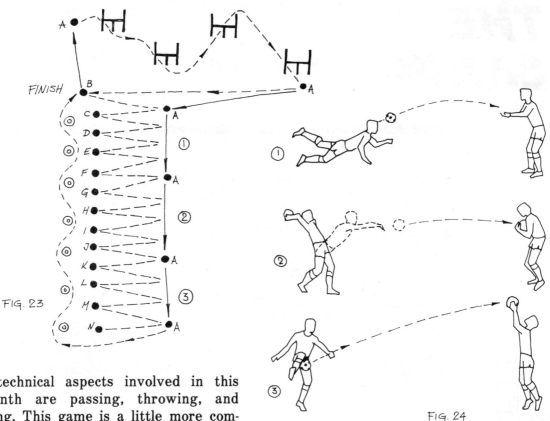

FIG. 23

FIG. 24

The technical aspects involved in this labyrinth are passing, throwing, and heading. This game is a little more complicated than the first labyrinth so it is important for the players to become familiar with its various parts before putting the parts together.

We begin by setting up a series of barricades formed by two chairs facing one another. They are set at a distance that should be determined by how experienced you and your teammates are. The player uses a trot or jog to approach the chairs, all the while dribbling the ball. When he comes to the chairs he passes the ball underneath them and then he himself jumps over them. He recovers the ball on the other side and proceeds to do this with all the chairs in the formation (see Fig. 23).

When he finally arrives at the last set of chairs he executes a pass to Player B and then runs to Post 2. Player B then returns the ball to Player A using his hands to do so. Player A then uses a diving position to head the ball back to Post 1 where Player C is located. He continues heading to Players D and E. From Player F to Player I he practices the overhand throw-in technique. Players J through N return the ball using their hands to do so. At the final stage of this drill, Player A dribbles to the left of Post 1 where there is a series of cones around which he must pass the ball. The finish line is where Player B is standing.

The game continues with Player B going through the labyrinth. In general, this is not a fast-moving game for the majority of players because they are in stationary positions. As a variation, Labyrinths I and II can be combined.

THE
STAIN

This game is an adaptation of tag, where one player touches another with his hand. The tagged one should, with one of his hands covering the part of his body that was touched (or "stained"), pursue the others until he can in turn touch them and put the stain on them.

In adapting the game for soccer, a ball is used to touch the other players. The pursuer can either throw the ball with his hands or kick the ball with his feet in order to tag the player.

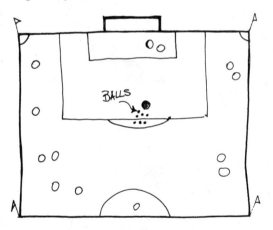

The field should be fairly large, if possible. This game can be played in a schoolyard, on a football field, or on the beach. Use half of the field if possible and begin the game with eighteen to twenty players. This is an ideal game for building up endurance because it demands that players continually run to try to escape.

Playing on the beach is excellent for strengthening leg muscles. If you do play on the beach be sure to adapt the game by throwing the ball with your hands — but remember the tag is valid only when it touches the legs.

To begin there is one player in the middle of the field with a ball at his feet. On the field there are as many balls as players lying around until someone picks them up. The rest of the participants voluntarily scatter around the field. With an indication from the coach, Player A begins to pursue the rest of the players who cannot run out of the bounds of the playing area. When Player A believes it is the opportune time, he throws the ball at the lower part of the opponent's body — from below the torso to the feet. If he succeeds in touching someone with a ball then that person is "stained" and joins Player A in a chase by picking up a ball from the field and pursuing players who are now his opponents. When only one player remains he is the winner.

A variation of this game is to play so that only one person is tagged at a time. When he is tagged, he becomes the only pursuer. Another variation is to start with Player A in the middle. He tries to tag the other individuals with his hand and when he does they both hold hands and begin pursuing the others until there is only one who remains and he is the winner.

MAYA
SOCCER

18

The Mayans lived in what is now southern Mexico and Guatemala. One of the games they liked to play was with a ball made of rubber. The game was violent (the losers were killed) but the game itself was interesting and consisted of making a ball pass through a small hoop which was attached high up on one of the walls of the yard where they played. These stadiums are still preserved as they were in those times; they even still show the trophies that the winning teams received. The players were treated as heroes.

This is a good game to play if the area where you are playing is small. Many times only a narrow corridor or an alley is available as a playing space — this game is perfectly suited to those conditions.

Five players is a good number for each team. That way everyone gets a good chance to play. For equipment you will need two hoops (hula hoops, bicycle hoops, or two old car wheels will all work) to use as goals. In the beginning, you place these hoops on the ground. The game basically is a soccer game but instead of regular rectangular goals the hoops are used — which serves to make the action more difficult. In time you will see how quickly the players find their way to the goal. At that point, you can raise the hoops to a height of 6 feet. Allow the players to score from both sides of the hoop. Play with a small, light

ball so that it will go through the hoop easily.

There can be two halves of play — each should be 20 minutes with a 5-minute break between them. You can organize a tournament giving two points for the winner, one point for each team in case of a tie, and no points for the loser.

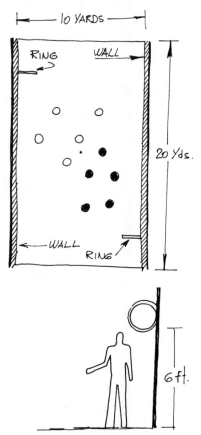

ONE
AGAINST ALL

19

In a way, this game is similar to dribbling through the New York subway at rush hour. Hard as it may seem, it's not impossible. And believe it or not, there's always someone in the crowd who can do it.

The playing area for this game should be an area that is 8 to 10 yards square. In the square are three defenders guarding the goal and one forward who begins the game with possession of the ball. In this game the defenders cannot ever enter the goal area. Each defender can individually attack the forward, but they cannot in pairs or as a group attack him. The forward tries to make a goal.

If a defender steals the ball, he has to pass the ball to the other two defenders. If he is successful the forward is out and another forward starts another game.

The forward can shoot into the goal from any place on the field; if he makes a goal the three defenders are eliminated and another three defenders take their place.

If a defender shoots and the ball goes out of bounds, then the forward must restart the game from the starting line, as in

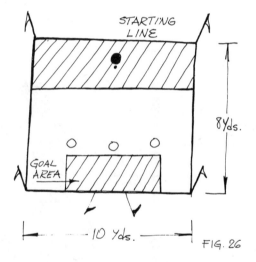

FIG. 26

Fig. 26. If the forward shoots and the ball goes out of bounds six times, he is out and another forward takes his place.

This game is very hard and I recommend starting with only two defenders in the beginning. When the players are more experienced you can make this game more difficult by making a rule that a goal can be made only from within the goal area. The best ball to use is the Number 3. One variation of this game is that if a defender steals the ball he then becomes the forward and the forward becomes the defender.

THE CORRIDOR

20

This game will look like a conveyor belt, always looking as if there's no end to it. The defenders are stationed on a long, imaginary corridor and the forward must run the length of the corridor to reach the goal on the other end, as shown in Figure 27. The defenders ready themselves one behind the other and try to block the forward from interrupting their chain.

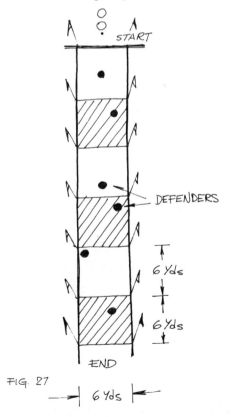

FIG. 27

To begin playing, mark the field with two lines that define the boundaries. The width of the field should be 6 yards and the amount of space between each defender should be about the same. The length of the field depends upon the number of players that you have.

Put a cone every 6 yards all along the length of the field. Put a defender next to each cone. The defender controls that area only and cannot enter any other area. The defender's job is to block the forward in his attempted passage through his area. If the defender is able to get the ball away from the forward he then becomes the forward and continues towards the goal himself. If he succeeds in reaching the goal, he wins points.

A variation of this game is this: If the ball is stolen from the forward by a defender he becomes disqualified and cannot play anymore, he can wait his turn and start again, or he can become a defender going to the end of the line and thereby creating an additional station.

If the defender in his dribbling shoots the ball out of bounds two times, the forward has the right to pass through the defender's zone without further interference from the defender. The forward can send the ball out of bounds twice only in each area.

67

THE DEFENDER

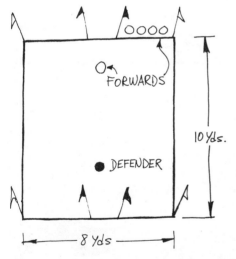

Defending an area is no easy task and it's even less so when a series of opponents tries to penetrate that area. This is an ideal game for strengthening dribbling skills, showing players how to take on an individual player (called a mark) and stimulating the defense at initiating the at-tack. It is exhausting but well worth the effort to play.

In a small field with two goals, two players face one another: one defender and one forward. The forward has possession of the ball. The forward tries to dribble into the defender's area to score. If he succeeds he forms a line behind the defense goal and waits his turn at being defender.

If the defender steals the ball or eliminates all the forwards who participate he wins the game. If the forward eliminates all of his opponents he wins the game.

This game is tiring especially for the defender so I recommend that you play for 3 minutes at a time. In the case of a tie the defender is the winner.

Both defender and forward can shoot out of bounds five times each. If they exceed this number they are eliminated. When a ball is out of bounds, each person restarts the game from his own goal area.

22

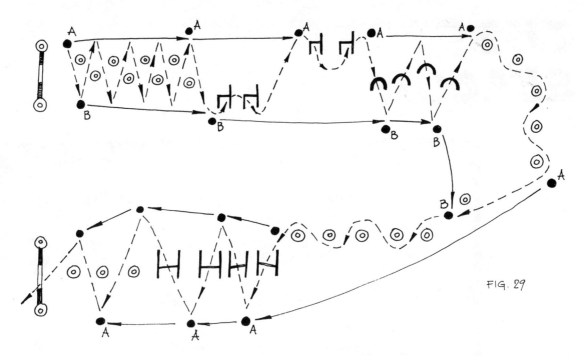

FIG. 29

One of the most basic and important things to teach all players about soccer is that it is a sport that requires teamwork and cooperation. This is not an easy thing to teach or to learn. It requires that people take care of one another on the field, that the relationship among all players is positive and nurturing. Goals are scored sometimes through exhaustive effort and exhaustive effort is activated by the player or players only when there is a positive group feeling among them. There are no stars or individual heroes in soccer; each man plays not for his own glory but for the benefit of all.

In this game it is apparent that what one does is fundamentally important for the other player. The outcome depends upon this attitude.

This game is played in pairs as you can see in Figure 29. The game consists of passing between one player and his partner with obstacles on the field. These obstacles can be cones, chairs, stakes, or hoops. The game begins with a series of passes between the cones. Each participant should pass the ball between the legs of two chairs, then through a series of hoops that have been tied to stakes. Then each participant will individually face a series of cones. He has to dribble around them and then pass the ball to his partner who must do the same. At this point they come to the stakes. They should practice an aerial pass at this station. The last station is a series of cones which are placed 1 yard apart on the field. This makes it difficult to pass but they must pass to one another on their way to the finish line.

The winners are the pair that spends the least amount of time performing this task. If you make technical errors you are penalized by having to repeat the task. The most important thing is to complete the circuit correctly because then there is benefit from the skills it teaches. Then you can begin to work on reducing the amount of time it takes to go through.

THE SLALOM

Working your way around an obstacle or a series of them is the object of this game. Team effort is important and you should be aware of the other players on your team so that your efforts can be coordinated with the others. This coordination will often make the difference between winning and losing.

The technical skills in this game are dribbling and learning good balance. It's necessary to change directions quickly in this game. It's played on a field that is marked in accordance with the skills of the participants — making it larger for the older, more experienced players.

Divide yourselves into two or three teams. A referee can keep track of when each team begins and when the last member of each team reaches the finish line.

Each team should have a captain elected by the participants; the captain will designate the order that the players are to go in. The first man of one team begins and every fifteen seconds another man from the same team should start. Each player has a ball and dribbles through the maze as fast and as effectively as he can. He cannot afford to go through quickly and carelessly because the person in back of him cannot pass him up. You'll get a good picture of the game by studying Figure 30. You can

make the stations more or less complicated to suit your teams.

Here as with other games, you can use different techniques of kicking and different balls, such as the medicine ball or a tennis ball, for variation.

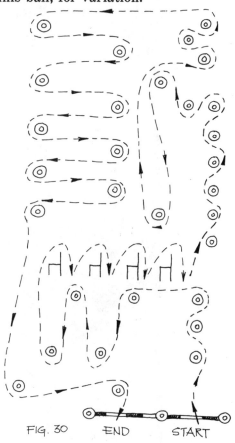

FIG. 30   END   START

HEADING

24

One of the techniques least common in soccer is heading. In the last few worldwide tournaments we have not seen many fine headers and it is apparent that the use of this technique is in crisis. I would nevertheless like to present to you an interesting game that can be played by two or four people that thoroughly covers all the necessary techniques of heading.

Heading is a technique that requires a great deal of practice. For beginners especially it is important that they overcome the fear and awe of moving the ball with their head. For many it is a natural instinct to avoid using the head, so I recommend, particularly for beginners, to go about this technique slowly.

If you play one against one, you really need very little space and Heading can be played indoors or outdoors. The advisable distance between opponents depends upon the skill of the players but normally is between 8 and 10 yards. The distance between members on the same team is between 4 and 6 yards.

Each pair of players heads and intercepts. To gain one point a person intercepts with his hands and then throws the ball in the air and heads it. To gain two points the person must head the ball directly back to his partner without first stopping or in any way touching the ball. To gain three points the players must dive for the ball with his head. (This is called head diving.) Each player can play for up to twelve points maximum, changing places with his opponent after he has reached six points. A time limit — 20 minutes each — is another way of scoring.

In the beginning it is better to use small soccer balls or rubber balls. An interesting variation to this game is this: have an opponent head the ball, stop it with his chest and continue playing with his feet in dribbling.

I feel the original game is better than the variation because it focuses on the technique; however in most cases the variation has more interest for the players, especially more experienced ones.

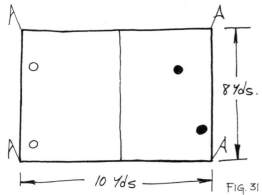

8 Yds.

10 Yds   FIG. 31

THE BRIDGE

The difference between a player with technical skill, and one with limited technical skill can be appreciated by seeing that the first always find a simple solution for any problem on the field.

Many times it is difficult to find a game suitable for three men to play but this is one of the best. The game consists of passing the ball from one to another over the defender. The defender, at first, is in a passive position, then semipassive, and finally becomes quite active. The defender tries to intercept the ball, and in doing so must use all available and legal moves to do it (see Fig. 32).

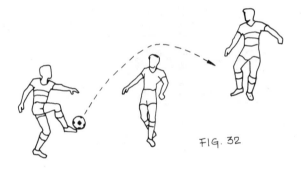

FIG. 32

To begin the players should place themselves about 20 yards apart. The defender is in the middle and cannot place himself nearer to one or the other. If he does intercept the ball he changes places with the last one who kicked it and the game resumes immediately. Variations to the game can be:

1. Limit the area of the game.
2. No limits on the area.
3. Limit the kicks.
4. Limit it to the use of one leg.
5. Use all the technical skills available such as heading and passing.

If one person is not as skillful as the other two, and spends too much time in a particular position, it would probably be best for him to rotate or to change his partners.

CIRCULAR HEADING

26

Acquiring the technical skills of heading is the main objective of this game. This is not a game for beginners because some control of the technique is required to gain adequate results. Young people may do this after about four or five years' experience in playing soccer.

Some coaches use this in their warming-up exercises before a practice or a game. It is very pleasant because it creates a cordial and fun environment before a game when everyone is usually quite nervous.

To play this game, pair up and face your partner. You should try to pass the ball from one to another using only your head. Then, after a certain amount of time, or when you can hit it eight or ten times without letting the ball fall, a third participant can be included (see Fig. 33).

The triangular figure formed by three

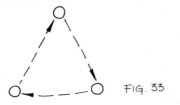

FIG. 33

players forces each person to move his head in the direction they wish to pass to. It also requires a certain amount of practice until you succeed in doing that. When you have mastered three players then you can incorporate another player to make four. Gradually the circle can be expanded even further to include a larger group (see Fig. 34).

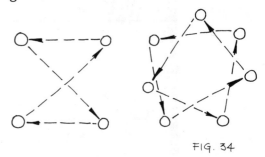

FIG. 34

For this I recommend using an uneven number of players; this way the circulation of the ball is better. The distance between the players can and should vary so the players can practice heading for long and short distances.

If you want to have a winner for this game, it can be that whoever loses the ball becomes eliminated until the final pair is selected.

JUGGLING

Juggling is used by professionals throughout the world. They use it as a warm-up exercise in the locker rooms, in hallways, in the minutes before a game begins. It appears very easy, and, in a way, it is. You must keep the ball in the air as long as possible before it hits the floor. To do this one can use any and all the known touches — the legs, the torso, the feet, the head — except for the hands.

This game can be played individually or in teams. You can keep score in the following ways:

1. Individual — count the touches until the ball hits the floor. (You can do this with or without a height limit.)

2. Teams — count the number of hits that the team acquires in a

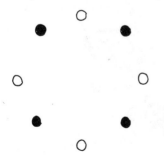

determined formation passing the ball from one to another.

3. Elimination — two teams play in the same circle. The one that lets the ball fall to the ground is eliminated. For this variation I recommend the use of a referee who can determine the person who committed the error. The team that eliminates the least number of players is the winner.

Another way to play is to mark the ground and the area that each player is to control.

To initiate beginners into this game I recommend an individual slow workout. If the participant has no experience, a variation such as "one and one" — which consists of helping one another with the hands — is useful. Another is an exercise more than a variation. The players bounce the ball on the floor in a one-bounce, one-touch rhythm, or have the player catch the ball with his hands. After the player has gained some confidence, eliminate the use of the hands or the bouncing on the ground. Following the process mentioned earlier, start in pairs, then in trios and so forth.

VOLLEY SOCCER

This can be a good game for practice on rainy days. It is an excellent game for any other kind of day in that the activity throughout the game is excellent physical work.

Generally it is played in places where volleyball is played. Almost all gyms have volleyball boundary lines already marked on the floor. If the people playing are very short the net can be lowered; otherwise it remains high.

This game can be played in teams made up of six players each. (see Fig. 36).

The rules of the game are: Each team can touch the ball only three times. If the ball touches the floor the other side gets it and scores. Any type of hit may be used to get the ball over the net except the hands. Each time the server changes the players rotate in the form that is marked with arrows as in volleyball.

If the players don't have enough experience with the ball this game will be too complicated. You may want to try it by changing some of the rules; for example, the number of times a ball can be touched can be changed from three to five. I recommend a reading of volleyball rules. When we acquire a certain amount of experience, we can limit the number of touches back to three, and use only one type of hit such as the instep or the head.

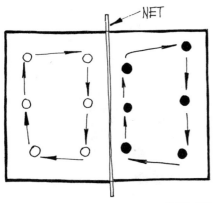

FIG. 36

BASKET SOCCER

29

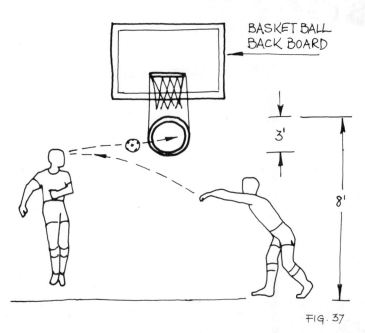

BASKET BALL
BACK BOARD

3'

8'

FIG. 37

This game is ideal for the rainy season when the fields are flooded and it's best to play indoors. This game is played in the same way that basketball is but there are two modifications. The first is that the hoop is not in a horizontal position — it must be vertical. The second change is that in order to make a goal, one must use the head.

For a goal use two hoops that can be hung from the backboard. Try to have the highest point no more than 8 feet off the ground, which is the regulation height of the goal. Because of this we can be sure that the forward will head the ball in the direction required for a normal goal, which is 8 feet in height. (See Fig. 37.)

If the players are children under twelve, use half of the basketball court or play seven against seven. Place the hoops on the backboard of the court. Keep the height of the hoop low by measuring the jumps of the participants and finding the average of the maximum and minimum height reached. This height should be the maximum height of the hoop. Use a Number 3 ball.

This game has a secondary purpose of showing off the tactical skills of passing, observing other players carefully, and learning how to receive the ball alone.

The movement of the ball on the court is with the hands. Using the hands offers the player a technical advantage which is easier, so that he may concentrate on the tactical aspects of the game (particularly observing other players).

To score the ball must pass through the hoop by heading it in. To do this the player must practice assisting (passing the ball to another player, and that player attempting to score a goal.)

TENNIS
SOCCER

30

Tennis Soccer presents itself as an important game in developing a sensitivity to touch, a sense of positioning on the court, and observing the opponent closely. The game is played on a tennis court and the rules are the same as they are for tennis. The size of the court does not allow for a powerful shot, because in doing this the ball would go out of bounds. A powerful shot could also permit interception using the head.

In general, the beginners believe that the force of the shot is most important; we see this a great deal in the professional games. When we see the applause, who is not to believe this? Potency is important, but more important is the aim; the precision in the hit, and the control of the technique. In this sense tennis soccer is a great combination in that it provides both.

This game can be played as in tennis, a singles match or a doubles match. The rules are the same as for tennis. For instance the ball can touch the ground only once; it can be hit (using different kicks, or by heading) before it touches the ground, or after. A point is scored if the opponent does not return the ball after it touches the ground or if the ball goes out of bounds.

If children play this game the coach can make the following allowances:

1. Allow the ball to bounce two or three times in the court.
2. Allow one or both people to pass the ball.
3. Allow each participant to hit the ball twice, or more if necessary.

All of these things facilitate controlling the ball. When the participants achieve a certain technical ability, then restrict these advantages.

SEASICKNESS

Preferred by all international players, I can without a doubt say that this is one of the most popular games around. It is an ideal game to begin practice sessions with, no matter what the technical level of the players may be.

This game may be played on any type of ground and the dimensions of the field have no importance. The same goes for the ball; it can be a small soccer ball, a tennis ball, or a regulation size ball. The rules are the same as for soccer. Two teams are formed with no more than three persons per team. (The teams should be balanced in accordance with technical and tactical capacity.) The game provides practice in dribbling, passing the ball with precision and learning to retain the ball for long periods.

You can play with or without goals. If you play with them, be sure that they are small (2 yards would be ideal). In some cases the game can be played with only one goal in which case the following rules should be observed:

1. The team that scores has the right to serve from its point of departure and they rightly have possession of the ball.

2. In the case of playing with two goals the departure point is executed by the team that scored from its goal line.

To make the game more difficult the coach can impose these rules:

1. Either one or two hits.
2. Obligation to pass the ball after having eluded one or two opponents.

The coach can control the duration of the game either by time or by goals. For example the team that gets the first six points wins the game. If it's done by time, keep in mind the level of training of the players. This is a game that demands great physical strength.

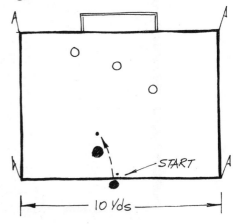

THE
IRON BALL

32

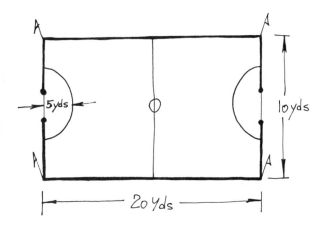

This enjoyable game is designed to pass the time and also exercise those muscles that we don't normally use. This can be played on any field, especially on lawn where the risk of injury by falling is reduced. All that you need is one ball and two goals that can be marked with two cones or flags. You can use the regulation ball or a medicine ball — though the medicine ball would probably be your best choice because its weight will help you develop your muscles. The game is a regular soccer game with a few variations:

1. The ball must be moved by rolling it on the ground.
2. The ball can be propelled with only one hand.
3. The ball cannot be touched with the feet.

4. When executing a pass with the ball and it comes off the ground, it is considered an error. The opposite team executes a free throw from the spot where the error was committed.

To effectively enjoy this game, I recommend dividing the teams in groups of no more than six people. In this way there is better circulation among the players in the game and everyone can enjoy it and get better exercise.

The time can be controlled by clocking it and dividing the game into two halves. There could be, for instance, two periods of 10 minutes each with a 3-minute break between them. You might choose to play for a determined number of goals — such as six or eight — and then change sides and take a break after one team has made half the goals needed to win.

In the course of the game you will see that the teams will appoint one man who practically places himself in the position of goalie. This can make scoring difficult. If you want to avoid this you can choose a semicircular area in front of the goal and prohibit anyone from going into it. If a forward penetrates the opponent's area he can be penalized as offside with an indirect free throw and the same if the defender penetrates his own area.

ENTER
GOAL WITHIN

33

When I was a child and arranged to play soccer in the school yard, the first of us to arrive would kill his boredom and impatience by hitting the ball against the wall until the second one came; then you could pass and dribble. But it became more interesting when the third person arrived. At that time we would make a goal with chalk on the wall, and a game would begin that now, forty years later, I remember with great nostalgia, because a great part of what I learned as a player I made into this game.

This game can truly be appreciated for its lack of a required place or equipment necessary to play it. Any ball can be used on any surface although as always I recommend grass.

To begin with, all you need are three players and a goal. One of the players should occupy the position of goalie (see Fig. 40).

The game begins in the following way: The goalie has possession of the ball, and the other two players are placed in corners A and B. At the signal, the goalie throws the ball towards the center of the playing field, and the two players start running to gain possession of the ball. In this way the game begins as a normal soccer game, with the same rules. The only difference is the moment when one of the players makes a goal. Then his opponent changes places with the goalie who now becomes the opponent.

This simple formula motivates the opponents to make a goal, and to watch closely who has possession of the ball. When the game is played two against two, or three against three with a neutral goalie, then the danger of losing the ball increases even more, and therefore makes the game more exciting.

In this variation, after the goal is made, there must be changes made in order to change the goalie:

1. Putting a number on each person, thereby preventing one player from playing goalie several times.
2. The last player to touch the ball from the losing team changes positions with the goalie.

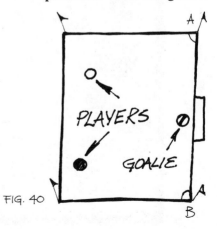

FIG. 40

JUGGLING II

34

Allowing the ball to become part of our body sounds like an idea from Zen. What I mean to say is that when we know something very well, when we have observed it closely, maneuvered and manipulated it, predicted its outcome — we have nearly become a part of it. That is what this game can do for the player.

In Juggling we find that the player eventually gains perfect control of the ball, using different touches such as the foot, the knee, the leg, and the head. To accomplish this, each man should have a ball and try to maintain that ball in the air (the ball cannot touch the ground) for as long as possible. The most important aspect is the attitude the player has toward learning to control the ball.

It is very important to learn how to concentrate on what one is doing. This concentration makes us observe our body: how it moves, how it responds to the ball, how it tells us something about the relationship between the two. Observing the ball, we see how it bounces, spins, rolls over itself, and it gives us an idea how to touch it. Its weight and velocity give us the elements that we need to feel its matter.

In observing our bodies we take note of which parts are tense, and which parts are relaxed, and the relationship that these elements have on the outcome of the ball — will it drop, or will it remain in the air?

If playing for individual points, the winner is the one who maintains the ball in the air the longest. Try playing with different types of balls such as rubber balls, plastic balls, or an orange. Better yet, play with a ball made out of paper. The important thing is to play, and see how many times you can hit it. You will see your progress in controlling the ball as if you were really a juggler.

ONE AGAINST ONE

35

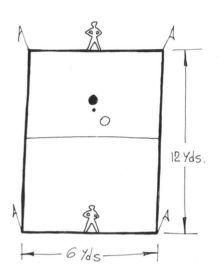

Basically the tactical problem in soccer is one player versus another and when this equilibrium is thrown off, one team has an advantage over the other. This game gives us the best chance to relate a player to the game. One of its important characteristics is that you can teach the two most important functions of the player: attack and defend.

In One Against One everything depends on you; this game works very well in changing the attitudes of certain players who don't like these two functions equally. Modern soccer demands of the players an attitude that defending is just as important as attacking. In this game we will find the best tool for that purpose.

This is played in small areas that should be marked with boundary lines and with goals. These can be replaced with two men who stand astride with their legs apart to form a goal. The goalies cannot use their hands. The game begins with each man in his respective goals; with a signal they go in search of the ball which is found in the middle of the field. The game can be scored by deciding on number of goals (six goals, for example) or playing by time — two halves of 3 minutes each with 2 minutes' interval.

You will see that this game demands great physical strength. It is why it is adopted by some teams for that objective while at the same time they work at the tactical and technical problems. The following rules can make the game less strenuous:

1. Change the pairs every one or two minutes.
2. Change the player who didn't score.
3. Play two minutes and rest one.

SHOOT OUT

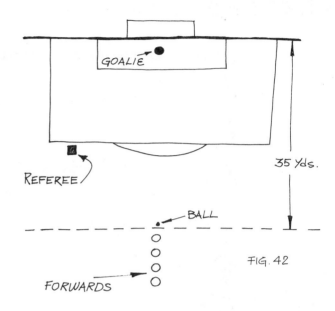

FIG. 42

Shoot out was a system used by the North American Soccer League to break the tied games in the United States. Even though there is much controversy surrounding this practice and many fans don't think it's fair to have the entire game decided by this single play, the game itself is interesting. It provides excellent technical training — particulary for the goalie.

The forwards learn to face the goalies, to become aware of their capabilities, and their limitations. The goalies learn to leave their areas, to cover the goal, and how to face the forward.

This should be played on a regulation-sized field. The forwards should be arranged in a straight line, each with his own ball. The forwards should be about 35 yards away from the goalkeeper, as you will see in Figure 42. With a signal from the referee, the forward begins his ad-

vance. He is granted only five seconds to make a score so it's important that someone be keeping time with a stopwatch.

The official rules allow only 5 seconds but I would recommend altering them in the following ways to accommodate the different skills of the players on your team:

1. Allowing an unlimited amount of time to score.
2. Allowing an unlimited number of touches.

These measures favor the forward and you will see that it will make his technical progress easier. Then you can come back to a more limited time and number of touches.

This game holds certain risks for the goalkeeper. He should wear protectors including shin guards, kneepads, gloves, and a plastic cup. The forwards should wear tennis shoes.

THE
NEUTRAL

This game is used daily in training professionals. It consists of putting fewer people on the defense team and more people on the offense thereby creating a situation where the defense (or offense, as the case may be) has to work harder at its job. The neutral is a middle fielder, and if possible, a man with experience who knows forceful offensive tactics. His duty consists solely of attacking, and he should do it at all times, because his mission is to support the team that possesses the ball.

Both teams can use known systems of play such as two versus two, three versus three and four versus four. They should wear shirts of different colors. For example if Team A wears yellow, Team B wears red, and the neutral wears green. If playing with people who have been well trained, the coach can place another player with the neutral one — especially when playing four versus four or five versus five (see Fig. 43). In this case I would advise using a field measuring 40 by 50 yards. The game can be played with or without a goalie without altering the development of the game.

If a goalie is not used, the width of the goal itself should not be more than 2 yards wide. The neutral only plays with the team that possesses the ball. That is to say that if Team A loses possession of the ball, the neutral immediately changes sides and plays with Team B until they score or until they lose the ball.

An interesting variation to this game is if the neutral only plays with the team that does not possess the ball. He plays in a defensive way. Another variation is to put the neutral on the offensive in the first half of the game and defensive during the second half.

As in other games, time periods can be of two halves 20 to 30 minutes each. Or the teams can play for a certain number of goals which may be (more or less) twelve. If the neutral player has experience in addition to tactical skills, he can really use these as an example to the whole team. In many cases, I would recommend that the coach play the neutral position, or if not, he should select the most intelligent player carefully and explain to him what it is that he is looking for — and work strictly with him.

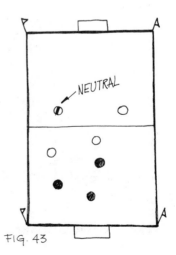

FIG. 43

SEVEN-A-SIDE

38

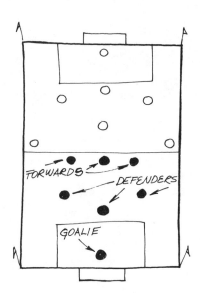

This game is excellent for school tournaments and for all-age children. It's one of the best-known drills of Rugby International, though in soccer we know it as "indoor soccer."

This game is ideal as a starter for children because it gives them the opportunity to see which position best suits them. Each position should be explained very clearly (hopefully by a coach or a teacher) and the two lines of forward and defense should be defined clearly. It's a good way for the participants to get an idea of order in covering the different areas on the field.

Each team consists of seven players: one goalie, three backs, and three forwards. The game is played in a small field that is usually about 50 yards in length. It can also be played in a gym or even on a basketball court. The game can be played with a Number 4 or Number 5 ball.

The rules of the game are the same as in soccer; the only differences are in the size of the field and the number of players.

In some places people play without boundary lines and the ball is still considered in play no matter how far afield it goes. This game is good because it gives the teacher, the parent, or the coach the opportunity to observe the players well.

In playing Seven-A-Side I advise that you play with one or two touches. With players who show skill in dribbling you may want to impose a limit on the number of touches or make an obligation to pass after having eluded the opponent. The secret of playing in a team is learning to pass the ball effectively; this is a good way of learning that skill.

THE SHIRT

39

Possession of the ball is one of the most important tactical factors in modern soccer. Nevertheless, we see very often that a team will lose the ball for a very small technical error — usually in the execution of a throw-in.

It is common for the ball to go out of bounds thirty or forty times during a professional game. This means that each team is performing a throw-in at least twenty times per game. Generally, it is the outside fullback who executes the throw-in, but all the players of a team should know how to do this perfectly. That is to say with power, aim, intelligence, and without technical errors.

To practice, hang a shirt on the cross-bar of the goal, and attempt to hit or knock down the shirt from outside of the penalty area. This is generally done after a day's practice. The one who succeeds gets to take his shower first. During summer practice, this reward has high incentive for the players.

The distance can be reduced or adjusted however necessary. We can start from the small area and add distance as we gain potency in the throwing.

An interesting variation for the goalies is in executing the throw with a medicine ball. This is an excellent workout — particularly for the arms and chest muscles. I consider this game both enjoyable and important for technique.

PING
PONG

40

The game of Ping Pong directly involves the technique of the throw-in, and complements The Shirt. This game can be played on any type of field or surface.

The game is developed in three areas. The center area is neutral. The number of players should depend on the age, height and technical skills of the players. To begin, I recommend playing in teams of four or five players. If coaching, be sure to instruct players in the throw-in technique (see Fig. 46).

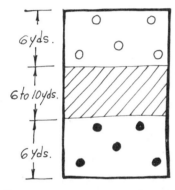

FIG. 46

The game consists of making the ball bounce into the opposing team's area by means of the throw-in. At first glance it appears quite simple, but I assure you that when the neutral area is quite wide, throwing-in becomes difficult. The amount of distance should be adjusted to meet the players' skills.

The direct tactical-technical benefits from this game consist of throwing correctly in the right direction and at the right speed so that your teammate receives the ball easily, can control it, and can then begin the attack.

I especially recommend playing this game on beaches to work on endurance. You may find it difficult to control the ball before it bounces on the ground so you can permit one bounce without penalty to make this game easier.

THE LITTLE HORSES

This is one game where it is important that it be played with adult supervision; you may find a parent, a teacher, or an older soccer-playing friend to serve as your coach.

One of the most important things in soccer training is building up strength in the player — particularly in the legs. The adult soccer player isn't affected too greatly by this because he's had a lifetime of working with weights or running or doing other things that will give him strength gradually. But you need to build strength gradually — not too fast and not too hard.

The Little Horses is a game that calls for plenty of running and is therefore an excellent way of building strength. The game involves creating a circuit of several chairs and cones. The participants then mount themselves on a teammate who then conducts the ball across the marked route until the team arrives at the marked point where there is a poster which says *change*. Now the person who rode will become the horse and will conduct the ball back down the course with the rider on his back, dribbling between the cones.

This game demands great physical effort. The length of the course should be determined by the age and strength of the players. There should also be enough space around the players to avoid accidents that might happen if they tripped or fell against one another. This game could eventually be included in the warm-up exercises of any team.

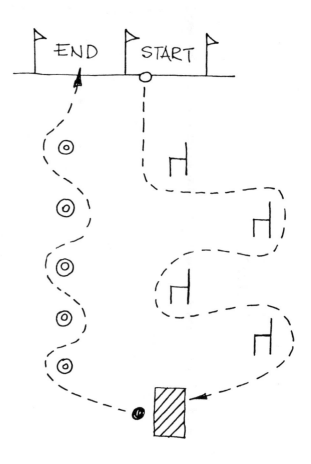

THE HUNTER

42

The Hunter is one of the most popular games in soccer and is played all over the world. You see it during practice sessions and during training, in the dressing room and in the park. It's a great game for warm-up. It emphasizes the ability to intercept passes, a skill that is known as "marking."

To play you need a very small space and at least three players. The rules are simple. The players are arranged in a circle with 3 or 4 yards between each. A defender is positioned in the center of the circle. The players must pass the ball to one another and try to keep the defender from getting it.

If the ball goes out of bounds the player who kicked it out changes places with the defender. The defender is apt to get very tired and you can limit the number of times a player can touch the ball to once or twice, which will make passing more difficult. The fewer the number of touches, the more difficult the game will be.

Another variation is for the ball to be passed in only one direction. This will force each player to kick with accuracy. When a pass is intercepted, the last player to touch the ball must change places with the defender.

The distance between the players is very important. If you have more than eight players in your circle it would be best to either form another circle or to add another defender. The position of the players will remain stationary and the defender will be the one to move around.

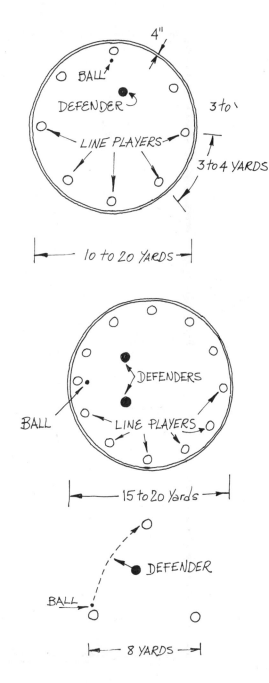

SOCCER
IN LINE

43

This is an ingenious game which will improve your ability to pass. It can be played on any surface — in the soft grass or on the hard floor of the gym. The size of the field should be relatively small, as shown in Figure 48.

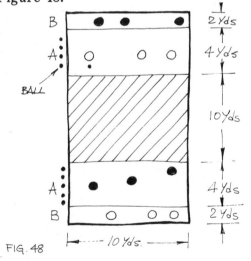

FIG. 48

Basically the game consists of passing the ball to teammates who are situated in the end zone. They in turn pass to their teammates. The game begins with one ball from the team that successfully draws the winning straw and is called Team A. They try to get their ball to their teammates who are in Zone B. If Team A is successful, it scores a point. If the players in Zone B return the ball, they get a point plus one-third point as a bonus.

There is a possibility that the opposite team will intercept the ball and if they begin a series of passes back and forth, they could end up with three points.

If Team A begins the first game, Team B should begin the second and alternate. Team B begins the second game no matter which team won the first.

Soccer in Line can be played by imposing time limits as well. The players of a team may pass the ball among themselves as much as they want to as long as they stay in their own zone. Once the ball crosses the line a team gives up control of it. If the ball goes out of bounds, another game starts by using another ball and going on to the team whose turn it is to start.

It might be best to start with ten balls and lay them out by the sides of the field. You can vary the passes (such as using passes in the air only) to add variety to the game.

THE
TWO PATIOS

44

One of the hardest things to learn in soccer is to hold your position and not to follow the ball while it is in motion. It's a question of patience versus impulsiveness — learning to hold back and keep your position so that when the ball comes your way you will be ready to act upon it.

The Two Patios will help you think about your relationship to the ball. The game needs two teams with six players each. Three players should occupy half of the field. These three players cannot cross over to the other side; if they do, it is an error and the opposite team will be awarded a free kick. You can see by studying Figure 49 that this creates an interesting inequality: three forwards must face only two defenders and the goalie. Therefore, the task of the defenders becomes more difficult than that of the other players.

You may also change the number of defenders. For example, there may be four defenders and only two forwards, as shown in Figure 50. This produces an equilibrium of man to man and a difference in the balance of the team. The team in black possesses more power in the attack, while the team in white has a greater number of defenders.

Variations can be made by moving people and changing their jobs. Another interesting variation is to play with one or two touches to help the ball circulate faster.

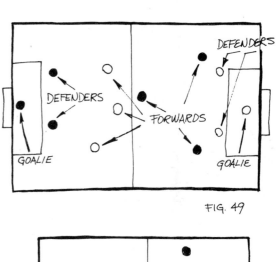

FIG. 49

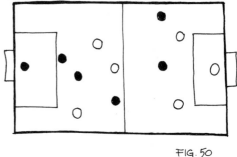

FIG. 50

WALKING
SOCCER

45

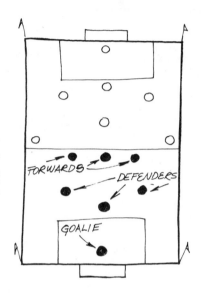

This is one of the most enjoyable games there is. It is no more than just running and escaping to open spaces; and speed is really not a factor in winning.

The participants learn what is called the "athletic march." One should play where there is ample space, so that players can really move their arms, and move about in general.

Participants discover how important position is on the field, to learn to move around looking for empty spaces to receive the ball, and to pass it — all while walking. They then discover how important it is to position themselves carefully because the ball moves more rapidly than the men.

When playing under normal soccer conditions, the speed of the action doesn't really permit the players to see the errors. In this way of playing they are concen-

trating too much on keeping up. In this game, however, it is a different matter. It is as if a movie were being shown in slow motion — because the errors become all too apparent to the players.

For the players being relieved of the desperation of not being able to run fast enough and get ahead of the ball, allows them to think of what should be done. This is where the will to win begins.

This game is interesting to try because it is a game not only meant for young people, but it tests the best of the pros.

The rules to play are simple: if you break into a run it is a foul and the opponent team gets a free kick. The rest of the rules are the same as in a regular soccer game.

THE
SQUARE TILE

46

Very few people doubt that the South American player possesses the highest technical level when it comes to controlling the ball and dribbling. Wondering how a player arrives at that level of competency and skill has made me watch these players carefully over the years. I've encountered the same answer in all the countries I've visited on the Latin American continent. The Latin player learns to play soccer as a child from four or five years old — either barefoot or wearing tennis shoes. He usually plays with very small balls which demand rapid movements, and he therefore develops a great sensitivity in his feet. To control those small balls of rubber demands great physical control, balance, and speed in reflexes. In general these children don't use regulation balls or regulation fields until they are ten or twelve years old. They learn to play in school yards, in the street, and many areas in which they play are quite small.

These very conditions (reduced space, many people, and small balls) are the same as in the game called The Square Tile. Let's begin by dividing the group into teams, and use the classic ways one versus one, two versus two, three versus three, or two versus one, three versus two, and so forth. Remember that when there are more than three people on the field, some players don't come in contact with the ball as easily. Notice this, and if it occurs, simply reduce the number of players on the field. If you have three versus two divide the group to form two versus one, and one versus one. This way assures a more effective workout in dribbling for the players (see Fig. 51).

To begin playing mark the field to measure 7 feet square and place the men on it. Either bounce the ball on the field to begin the game or give the ball to the team

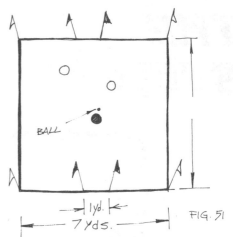

FIG. 51

with the least number of players.

This game can be played with or without goals. I think it is more interesting with goals. Use small balls, tennis balls for instance. Play two halves of 5 minutes each for players under twelve. It is better to play for a certain number of goals attained, perhaps six, and then change sides.

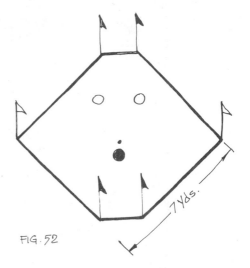

FIG. 52

An interesting variation to this game consists of marking the field in the form of a rhombus (see Fig. 52). In this way the players dribble with more effort and concentration because the shape of the field is a new dimension for them.

THE STICK

47

What often seems to be a simple game or a simple maneuver turns out to be more difficult than it looks. This game is no exception. The technical aspects of this game are dribbling and taking the mark. Once again it is the eternal drama of soccer: one against one. The forward has the sole objective of touching the stick with the ball and thus scoring; the defender also has one objective — trying to destroy the intention of the forward.

To begin playing all that is needed is a stick and one ball. If desired, a circular zone can be marked on the field for the defender who cannot come out of that zone.

This game is probably one of the most interesting ones for learning how to take the mark and how to dribble. The defender learns that it is very important to look in back of himself often, to steal the ball if possible and to block his opponent in the execution of a pass. If his opponent does attempt a pass, then the defender should try to intercept the ball.

For the forward who learns to dribble expertly and elusively around a man, the main objective is to try to get his opponent out of the line so that he can then make a pass and touch the stick.

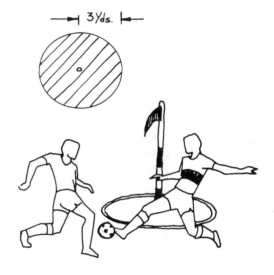

In general, this game is played with one hit of the stick and when this occurs defender and forward change positions. The first one to earn five points is the winner. Another way of changing positions is that the defender can steal the ball from the opponent and, if he succeeds, he can himself hit the stick with the ball and thereby score. This game can be played on any kind of surface, including playgrounds and gyms, using any kind of ball.

THE SPIDERS
AND THE BIRDS

48

Training shouldn't always have to be hard work and you shouldn't always have to be thinking about what direct benefit the exercise you are doing is having on you. Sometimes it's more important just to laugh and enjoy yourself — and be happy for the friendship that comes out of the game.

The Spiders and the Birds is a game that does demand tremendous physical effort, especially in the legs, arms and the abdominal muscles. You play on a relatively small field — one measuring 7 by 7 yards will do — and you can play three against three or two against two, as shown in Fig. 54. The Spiders play sitting down and can move around only in that position. The Birds play standing on their feet and can use any touch except for handling the ball with their hands. The Spiders can use any part of their bodies including their hands.

The Birds' object consists of making a goal and for this they can use as many balls as there are players on the field. The Spiders, on the other hand, are interested only in defending the goal. They try to steal the balls away from the Birds and send them out of bounds. For this they can only use their fists. The game is over when

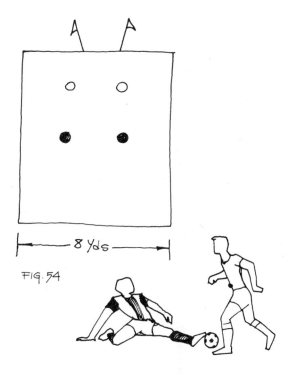

FIG. 54

8 yds

the Birds score one point. They then leave the field and a new team comes on to take on the Spiders. If the Spiders get all the balls away from the Birds then they are the winners and will take on the challengers, who will come on as Spiders. The old Spiders will then become Birds.

THE PENDULUM

49

I remember that when I was a child I'd go out and hang an old ball that my grandfather had given me on a crossbar and for hours I exercised different touches, especially with my left leg. It was because one of the best players and coaches that Argentina had, Don Renato Cesarini, had told me, "He who cannot manage the two legs with the same ability will not be able to play anywhere." This was in the 1940s and it's now clear that Don Renato knew what he was talking about. He was one of the first players that Argentina had exported to Italy during the 1930s. (This game is in a way an homage to the man who introduced modern soccer to my country.) The Pendulum was one of his favorite games and is, without a doubt, one of the best and most economical, in terms of time and money, ways at working all the technical aspects.

When a player does not have good technique and wishes to improve it, all he needs is a ball, a rope and you're ready to begin practicing. Also, if you prefer you can fasten the rope on some part level on the ground.

The important thing in this game is not to lose any time; the second the ball returns to you, be ready for it.

This way you can also practice reception and mix a kick with a reception at the same time.

The possibility of raising or lowering the ball offers these and all possible variations (see Fig. 55).

Some teams in South America used to have a series of four to six pendulums to use during their training. They are situated in the rear of the field so that the players can practice different kinds of heading or kicks.

If you wish to compete in this, you should count the technical errors as point against you. In this way the player with the least number errors is the winner of the game. Also, you can place the best player in a technical category by age:

1. Champion of the interior instep.
2. Champion header.

The Pendulum is the best manner in which to train. The difficult techniques immediately capture your attention and motivates you to excel.

This way you become interested and learn our philosophy which is to find the best talent in each one of us and improve it.

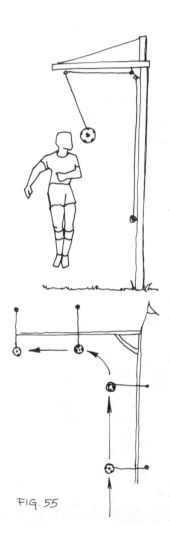

FIG. 55

FULBITO

50

Fulbito has become to my country what Monopoly is to the U.S. In some countries in Europe they sell beautiful sets with the players done very realistically to allow you to play this game of "indoor soccer." My experience with the game is more romantic, however. It evokes a time when a piece of plywood painted green was the field of Wembley in England, or the stadium of River Plate in Buenos Aires, where the coat buttons are the idols we admire on T.V., daily publications, and magazines. With all this magic we see ourselves playing with Pelé, Cruift or the Argentina team.

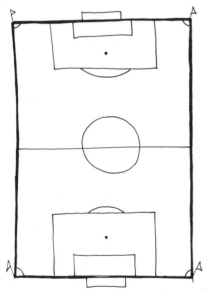

If you believe in this get a piece of plywood that measures 36 by 48 inches and draw a soccer field the best you can. You will need eleven buttons for each team. It would be best that they be clearly different. You can use model airplane paint or colored fingernail polish. The important thing is that the two teams look totally different on the playing field. One can be white and the other red.

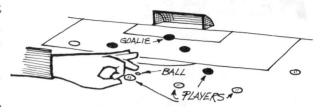

For each team, place in the field eleven players and then drop a ball (a smaller button) in the middle of the field. The ball will fall near a certain player and this determines who starts the game.

The team possessing the ball begins a continuing series of passes until they consider they are in a position to score. (This can be from any place on the field.) If the shoot goes out of bounds the opposite team begins the game with a goal kick.

The same rules are observed as in a regular soccer game. The only difference is that there is no possibility of moving the players when the ball is in movement. You can move three players when the ball is out of bounds and one when you are playing, but before the ball is acted upon. To move the players use the index finger or a pencil. Keep in mind that when one player touches another it is a foul and a free kick is awarded; if this occurs in the penalty area it is a penalty kick. You play with offside and it is penalized with an indirect kick. (See the rules of the game).

You should have the goalie be heavier than the rest. You can glue a coin on the bottom part. This extra weight will prevent the shot from knocking him down.

The imagination will do the rest. I recommend that you read the chapter covering the rules of the game so that these modifications make sense with the original rules. Always remember that these games are for enjoyment so use them for that and enjoy.

Conclusion

When I was an art student in Buenos Aires, I had a professor who taught me sculpture. He was really a very simple man who, at the same time, was quite profound. After the class ended — at around 11 PM — we would all go out for coffee and continue asking questions. Many times these discussions would go on until after midnight.

I remember one night I asked him two questions that were answered in such a way as I'll never forget. The first was this: *How do you obtain a personal style?* This is what my teacher, Antonio Sassone, said, "A personal style is something that you cannot avoid. Everything that you do — and don't do — is a product and expression of your personality. This isn't just in your artistic activity but in whatever else you do."

My second question was this: *How does one know that he is on the road to his vocation?* He answered, "Simply because one does not notice the sacrifices that a career demands. They are done with pleasure and are almost like a game. You *like* doing them."

Time has passed since those talks with my professor but they still hold a sweet flavor in my memory. With time I've come to understand the scope of his words and to realize that they apply to soccer as much as they do to art. When a soccer player practices, his devotion to the game and the personal way that he goes about playing it have everything to do with him as an individual.

In this book there is much that my professors have shown me. I hope I have had the chance to transmit their knowledge to you.